BULLETPROOF MASTERCLASS

BY LAURAINE WHITE

CONTENTS

CONTENTS

BULLETPROOF

SECTION 1: WELCOME

Lauraine

MEET YOUR INSTRUCTOR

Author of:

- Chosen
- The Way Out
- Bulletproof
- and many more titles to come!

She is an entrepreneur, real estate broker, former pastor, and lover of Jesus. She's also the mother of three children. loves to sing, cook and travel.

Contact me on:
+1 770.912.3894
lwhite@miracle-movement.com

A WARM
WELCOME

DEAR FRIENDS

Thank you for purchasing this material and taking this journey of discovery with me. Some of this information you may have seen or heard of before but some of it you may not have. The goal is to open yourself to this process.

We invite you to see the Trinity: God the Father, Jesus, the Son, and the Holy Spirit in new ways by allowing the Holy Spirit to breathe new understanding in you. If you've never encountered the Holy Spirit, we invite you to learn who the Holy Spirit is, how He works, and why you need Him. Don't get caught up in the gender roles I've placed. The Holy Spirit is Spirit and no gender role can confine who He is. It's bigger than that. So if you call Him something other than Him, I'm okay with that and so is Holy Spirit. The point is to just call on Him-- however you are led to do so.

Today is your day. So, lay aside the distractions and other things that get in the way of you experiencing God in a whole new way. I am so excited about your future!

Lauraine E. White

ACHEIVE YOUR GOALS!

HOW DO I QUALIFY?

How, then, can they call on the one they have not believed in? And how can they believe in the one of whom they have not heard? And how can they hear without someone preaching to them? And how can anyone preach unless they are sent? As it is written: "How beautiful are the feet of those who bring good news!" Romans 10:14-15

I want to give insight as to how I gained knowledge of this material and why it's important for you to understand the depth of my experiences.

This journey for me began September 11, 2001 when I was placed on a road of discovery where I learned the art of spiritual warfare through the things that I suffered within my home. Demons moved into my house and took over my family. Satan got in bed with me every night disguised as my husband.

I had whip marks on my back for months and knew that I was under attack but I had no one to teach me what I was going through. Until I encountered an angel at my workplace.

She taught me how to fast and pray. She enlightened me on demons and how they work. She gave me insight on why Satan hates us so much and that he doesn't fight fair. But the fight for us is fixed so we don't fight like the world does when it's at war. "The weapons of our warfare are not carnal, but mighty through God" (II Corinthians 10:4)

At the end of our 40-day fast, I watched demons literally leave my husband's body. As they did, he was left, gripped with guilt and paralyzed from all the pain caused through Satan running amok in his life.

Every obstacle that came my way led me to seek God more--not less. I knew God was my only answer and I was desperate for a way out.

My seeking led me to two bishops from two different cities but who ended up in Atlanta looking for real estate. That's how our lives collided, but God had a greater plan.

They gave me the opportunity to gain practical knowledge on spiritual warfare. Living daily with such great men of God was a privilege that only God could've afforded me, but little did I know that God wanted to use my gifts to send a message to these two anointed leaders regarding idol worship and the spirit of Eli.

I didn't seek God first. He was seeking me. And as God was getting my attention, Satan pulled out his big guns to destroy God's original plan for my life.

It didn't work. I'm still here and I'm still in pursuit of what God has for me. Nothing else matters.

After delivering God's message to these bishops, which frankly still overwhelms me because they both abandoned me. I was left alone. That's when the Master teacher, comforter and best friend, Holy Spirit, stepped in, raising a standard against all that came against me and my household.

Looking back over my life, I don't regret any of my steps. They led me to know God in ways that I never dreamed of. He taught me how to mark, hear and understand His voice.

He gave me a boldness, not brashness to stand in the face of those that oppose God and me and speak what God gave me. I learned to decree over circumstances, policies, and governmental order and watch God change them.

Before God could use me, He had to empty me of religion, and the filth of who I became because of my association with it.

As we begin this journey together, I want to encourage you to reflect on where you've been and seek Holy Spirit's direction on what you need to discard and what to keep. Your steps were ordered to this place so don't miss what He has for you.

"The journey of a thousand miles begins with one step." Lao Tzu

MISSION STATEMENT

We exist to educate, motivate, and inspire those seeking to know God in a deeper way. We help these seekers to build a relationship with Jesus that goes beyond church attendance, singing in a choir or serving on a church board. Furthermore, we establish with seekers of divine knowledge understanding their identity in Christ, who their enemy is, and how to endure the battles of life. This is accomplished by orchestrating tried and true life strategies that involve prayer, fasting, and the greater works being firmly rooted in them. We believe that miracles, signs and wonders follow us because Jesus's spirit lives in us; therefore, the greater works are done through us.

MIRACLE-MOVEMENT.COM

SECTION 2: INTRODUCTION

"Arise, shine, for your light has come,
and the glory of the Lord rises
upon you.
See, darkness covers the earth
and thick darkness is over the
peoples,
but the Lord rises upon you
and his glory appears over you.
and kings to the brightness of your
dawn.

ISAIAH 60:1-3

INTRODUCTION

Read chapter 1: Shooters in "Bulletproof" companion book.

But seek ye first the kingdom of God, and his righteousness; and all these things shall be added unto you. Matthew 6:33 KJV

One of the Fetzer Institute research projects done in 2020 on spirituality found that 9 out of 10 adults in the US consider themselves to be spiritual, religious or both. 1 in 6 claim to be spiritual instead of religious.

What does it mean to be spiritual? This is an extensive topic and is subjective based on each individual's perception. But for most people, it is the idea or belief in something or someone beyond or greater than themselves.

For some people, it goes further by answering questions about creation, where do we come from, how did we get here, can we trust the bible and what will the end look like?

Spirituality for many is a journey and not a destination. It's all in their approach to the subject matter.

BULLETPROOF MASTERCALSS

The Research

Half of those who identify as spiritual but not religious—or neither spiritual nor religious—grew up in a religion, but left religion.

Focus group and survey participants described the complexities, nuances, or limitations of labeling themselves according to religious or spiritual identities.

Religious Consistency

	[R] [S] Religious & Spiritual	[S] Spiritual only	[R] Religious only	Ⓡ Ⓢ Neither	% summary based on all responses
Same religion	73%	25	62	34	Same religion **61%**
Different religion	19	26	13	15	Different religion **20%**
Found religion	2	3	2	1	Found religion **2%**
Left religion	6	47	23	50	Left religion **18%**

Source: 2020 Study of Spirituality in the U.S., survey conducted Jan. 16 - Feb. 3, 2020, Fetzer Institute.

Religious consistency was determined by comparing how respondents identified their religion growing up with their religion today. (1) Same religion: If respondent answered "present religion" and "religion growing up" as same religion. (2) Different religion: If respondent answered "present religion" and "religion growing up" as different religion. (3) Found religion: If respondent answered "present religion" as any religion, and "religion growing up" as Atheist, Agnostic, or Nothing in particular. (4) Left religion: If respondent answered "present religion" as atheist, agnostic, or nothing in particular, and "religion growing up" as any religion.

Earls, A. (2021, February 3). Most Americans embrace religion, spirituality-even atheists. Lifeway Research. https://Research.lifeway.com/2020/09/24/most-americans-embrace-religion-spirituality-even-atheists/

BULLETPROOF MASTERCLASS

The Research

Many people who don't identify with any religion today still consider themselves spiritual to some extent.

Participants who described themselves as not at all religious did not necessarily label themselves agnostic, atl or "nothing in particular." Neither did they all disaffiliate from religion: Some focus group and interview particip who said they were not religious still named a religious denomination.

"To what extent do you consider yourself a spiritual person?"

	Nothing in particular	Agnostic	Atheist
Very [S]	12	4	1
Moderately [S]	25	21	15
Slightly [S]	34	35	18
Not at all (S)	27	40	66%

% summary based on all responses

Very spiritual
23%

Moderately spiritual
39%

Slightly spiritual
23%

Not spiritual at all
14%

Source: 2020 Study of Spirituality in the U.S., survey conducted Jan. 16 - Feb. 3, 2020. Fetzer Institute.

Earls, A. (2021, February 3). Most Americans embrace religion, spirituality-even atheists. Lifeway Research. https://Research.lifeway.com/2020/09/24/most-americans-embrace-religion-spirituality-even-atheists/

"

"TO SEDUCE THE
ENEMIES' SOLDIERS
FROM THEIR
ALLEGIANCE AND
ENCOURAGE THEM
TO SURRENDER IS
OF SPECIAL SERVICE,
FOR AN ADVERSARY
IS MORE HURT BY
DESERTION THAN
BY SLAUGHTER."

- FLAVIUS VEGETIUS RENATUS

SPIRITUALITY OVER RELIGION

Those who consider themselves to be spiritual are seekers of the higher good. They believe that we are all interconnected with all of humanity, including being one with nature. Some will live out this understanding through their religious practices and others deny that religious practices are necessary to experience this place of higher good.

Spirituality is as varied as cultures are. We should not only look at our differences, but pay attention to what we have in common. We are all looking for:

- answers to questions on suffering, death and what comes afterward.
- meaning for our lives.

WHY NOT RELIGION?

The original intent of religion was to build community and so that we are not alone in our pursuit of God. But as with anything that is driven by man, corruption can enter in and alter the original plan to make it something unappealing. Unfortunately, the ulterior motives of a few bad players can spoil the whole bunch because once you've been bitten by it, you don't want any part of it in the future.

1. Matt. (n.d.). The State of Church Attendance: Trends and Statistics [2024]. ChurchTrac. https://www.churchtrac.com/articles/the-state-of-church attendance-trends-and-statistics-2023

THE SHIFT
Starting Over

According to churchtrac.com, "pre-pandemic, approximately 3,500 people left the religious congregations every day. That's a rate of 1.2 million walking away from church every year.... However, on average, churches are at 85% of their pre-pandemic attendance level."[1]

So we have 1 in 6 adults in the USA that feel that they needed to leave the church in order to become spiritual. How did this happen? Were there common circumstances that brought these individuals to make the decision that church could no longer feed them spiritually? Where is God in all of this?

WHAT CAUSED THIS SHIFT

According to *Psychology of Religion and Spirituality* (Van Tongeren et al., 2021), written by Aaron T. McLaughlin, Daryl R Van Tongeren, Kelly Teahan, Don E. Davis, Kenneth G. Rice, and C. Nathan DeWall, two studies were conducted to take a look at those who were once considered religious but are no longer a part of any religious organization. Out of this study and based on the participants' written narratives, the administrators of the study observed four common problems that were consistent among those who are out with religion.

In the survey of sacred experiences, a staggering 51.8% wrote that their reason for leaving was that their faith was no longer sufficiently meeting their intellectual needs. Around 21.9% of the participants bore scars of spiritual trauma, one of which was the jolting agony and disillusionment caused by the abhorrent sexual abuse scandals that plagued the Catholic Church. Approximately 14.9% cited personal struggles, such as grappling with the inexplicable loss of a child, while 11.4% attributed their departure to social factors, such as feeling ostracized or unaccepted within their religious community.

McLaughlin, A. T., Van Tongeren, D. R., Teahan, K., Davis, D. E., Rice, K. G., & DeWall, C. N. (2022). Who are the religious "dones?": A cross-cultural latent profile analysis of formerly religious individuals. Psychology of Religion and Spirituality, 14(4), 512–524. https://doi.org/10.1037/rel0000376

THE ALTERNATIVE

These numbers are staggering. When we consider that it was sixty years ago, in 1963, that prayer was taken out of schools, and in that timeframe, we have seen an increase in those that no longer believe that Jesus is our Savior. Is this a coincidence or part of a greater plan?

I believe it's a part of a bigger plan to keep us from having a personal relationship with God. One that is not predicated on doing all the right things, looking a certain way or other social constraints that are placed on us by society. No. I believe that there are forces at work trying to convince us that God does not love or care about us. Nothing could be further from the truth.

GOING DEEPER

What do you do when a door shuts, whether by your choice or forced by others? Do you linger around trying to get back in or do you look for another door? Do you wait to get clarity on what direction to take? Who do you depend on in times when you don't know what to do?

If you're like most people, when it comes to spiritual matters, we've relied on those we consider to be more enlightened, whether a parent, teacher,

16

coach, counselor or pastor, to help shape what we believe.

Seeking answers to life's struggles is a human dilemma and shouldn't be based on someone else's opinion on what is the truth of a matter. It requires asking relevant questions of someone whose life demonstrates that they've experienced God. But better than seeking human help, I encourage you to seek the answers you desire from the only one that can give you curated answers that were designed just for you.

Your life matters. It doesn't just matter to your family. It matters to God. He, on purpose, placed you on earth at just the right time to accomplish a unique set of plans. You thought those were your original ideas, but God is the originator of those plans. He performed a heavenly download to your mainframe before you were born so that you have all that you need to accomplish the goals He set for you.

Why does it feel like everything's going awry or is topsy turvy? Because, although God downloaded the plans, you still need Him to carry out the plans to perfection.

We're here to help you navigate this time of your life. Jesus is calling you to finish the work that He began in you. Whether you acknowledge Him or not. He wants a relationship with you and to be with you as you do the work that you were born to do.

TRANSFORMATION BEGINS HERE

To grow spiritually, we need a plan of action. We will use the following framework to help you produce your plan for effective change that will provide a road map to get you from where you are today to where God wants you to be.

CONTEMPLATION

Winston Churchill once said, "Fear is a reaction. Courage is a decision." In this phase, our contemplation needs to be more in line with courage, not fear.

- Where do you stand with regard to spiritual matters?
- Do you believe that Jesus is God's son? Why or why not?
- What brought you to this place?
- What life-changing shifts do you need to make to align with God's original plan for your life?

PREPARATION

In the Art of War, Sun Tzu states, "Plan for what is difficult while it is easy, do what is great while it is small."

- Tune in to your mindset and patterns toward spiritual matters.
- Pause negative thoughts and embrace the new information that will be presented here. Stay open to this process.
- Engage in the study of the material, with the group and on your own to allow the Spirit to give you insight on what is important to your development.

ACTION

"Begin with the end in mind." Stephen Covey

- If you haven't already, accept Jesus as your Savior.
- Forgive those that have hurt, disappointed, or intentionally brought harm to you.
- If you have chosen to step away from religion or haven't decided whether or not Jesus is your Savior, open your heart to hear the Truth of who Jesus is and what He really wants from you.

18

"I took another walk around the neighborhood and realized that on this earth as it is—
The race is not always to the swift,
Nor the battle to the strong,
Nor satisfaction to the wise,
Nor riches to the smart,
Nor grace to the learned.
Sooner or later bad luck hits us all."

Ecclesiastes 9:11

NOTES

NOTES

SECTION 3: PREPARATION

"LIFE IS LIKE BAKING BREAD. IT'S THE *YEAST* THAT YOU PUT IN IT THAT CAUSES IT TO RISE."

Laurnine White

PREPARATION

ASSOCIATIONS

Does everyone in your circle wish you well? Jesus warned His disciples against their associations. In Luke 12:1, He says, "Be on your guard against the yeast of the Pharisees, which is hypocrisy." Yeast, deposited in a ball of dough will cause it to rise when cooked. Yeast changes the composition of the flour when mixed together in water. In the same way, corrupt associations do the same to us. Their deposits, of which they are, when mixed with who we are, cause us to change. The Word of God, in Amos 3:3 says, "Can two walk together except they be agreed?" Either you will influence them, or they will influence you if you don't already have the same properties of "leavening" in you.

- You must be baptized in water and by the Spirit. John 3:5 NASB: Jesus answered, "Truly, truly, I say to you, unless someone is born of water and the Spirit, he cannot enter the kingdom of God."

- Guard against evil associations

24

"Be on your guard against the yeast of the Pharisees, which is hypocrisy." Luke 12:1

In your relationships, is there more competition than teamwork?

"Life is like an obstacle course relay race. There are hurdles and tunnels and you believe that it's about your abilities but it's more about who your alliances are."

Lauraine White

Birds of a
FEATHER FLY TOGETHER

YOUR ASSOCIATIONS

Who are the people that you are connected to that influence your thinking about life, including spiritual matters?

- ☐ Family: Parents, siblings, aunts, uncles, cousins
- ☐ Friends from High School
- ☐ Friends from college
- ☐ Business associates
- ☐ Neighbors
- ☐ Community affiliations
- ☐ People met socially
- ☐ Fraternity brothers/sisters
- ☐ Friends met at social clubs/parties
- ☐ Social media network

DO YOUR FRIENDS SINK YOUR SHIP?

DO THEY ANCHOR YOU TO PROBLEMS OR DO THEY LEAD YOU TO SOLUTIONS?

TWO SIDES TO ANCHORS

ASSOCIATIONS

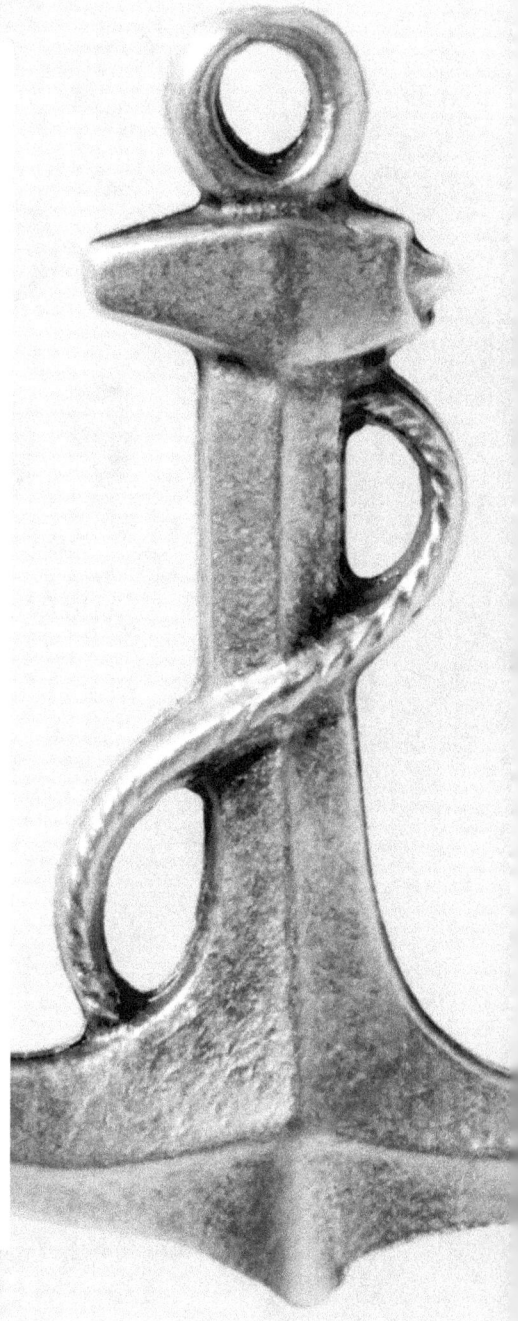

To understand the importance of anchors for ships at sea, we will discuss their use.

Anchors play a critical role in ensuring a ship's safety, keeping it from capsizing while pivoting around the anchor to face the wind. Even in the midst of a storm, the captain can rely on a sea anchor to serve the same purpose and keep the ship secure.

But if left in place, the anchor will keep the ship from moving ahead from it's stationery position. That's the negative side to connections that anchor us when we want to move forward.

The key is knowing who is a toxic or atoning anchor within your sphere of influence and put them in categories as you plan ahead. Just as you would add yeast to flour and water to cause the dough to rise, you must add people in your life that will help you as you rise.

"Can two walk together, except they be agreed?"
Amos 3:3

ANCHOR EXERCISE

Anchors are used in many applications, whether on a ship, in construction or in our lives, and they help to secure or create a stronger connection between two objects. This exercise will be used to identify the anchors in our lives and separate those that are toxic from those that restore.

TOXIC RELATIONSHIPS

RESTORATIVE RELATIONSHIPS

SOMETIMES THE TOXIC RELATIONSHIPS ARE FAMILY.

This exercise is not meant to encourage you to end all toxic relationships but to bring awareness so that you get to choose how to shape those relationships in the future.

31

"Birds of a feather, flock together," that's what my mother used to say. What she meant by that statement is that those of like character tend to group together.

It's unlikely that criminals will hang out with preachers. It's impossible for this to work because they don't see eye to eye, unless one has influenced the other.

When evaluating your associations, you will need to assess them based on where you're going from here. This will require you to be very intentional about where you've been and what's coming next. The goal is to end shipwrecking cycles and enter this season of opportunities leading to your destiny. You could be moments away from what God has in store for you. Are you going to let a few destiny destroying friends upend His plans?

KEY DECISIONS

- Which friends/ family will remain in your circle of influence?
- How will you change the relationships?
- Can you end any of these associations?
- Courage in the face of change is required to carry out these steps.

32

NOTES

NOTES

PREPARATION

REPENTANCE

Luke 3:8 – "Therefore produce fruit worthy of repentance. And do not begin to say to yourselves, 'We have Abraham as our father.' For I tell you that out of these stones, God can raise up children for Abraham." **Repentance produces:** (Ezekiel 36:25-27): "I will sprinkle clean water on you, and you will be clean; I will cleanse you from all your impurities and from all your idols. I will give you a new heart and put a new spirit in you; I will remove from you your heart of stone and give you a heart of flesh. And I will put my Spirit in you and move you to follow my decrees and be careful to keep my laws."

"Change does not roll in on the wheels of inevitability, but comes through continuous struggle." Dr. Martin Luther King, Jr.

REPENTANCE PRODUCES

A NEW HEART
Source: New Living Translation

According to Ezekiel 36:26: **And I will give you a new heart, and I will put a new spirit in you. I will take out your stony, stubborn heart and give you a tender, responsive heart.**

GOD'S SPIRIT
Source: King James Version

Luke 4:18-19: **The Spirit of the Lord is upon me, because he hath anointed me to preach the gospel to the poor; he hath sent me to heal the brokenhearted, to preach deliverance to the captives, and recovering of sight to the blind, to set at liberty them that are bruised, to preach the acceptable year of the Lord.** Also read Acts 2:38, II Timothy 1:7-9

POWER
Source: New International Version

Acts 1:8: **But you will receive power when the Holy Spirit comes on you; and you will be my witnesses in Jerusalem, and in all Judea and Samaria, and to the ends of the earth."** Also read Eph. 6:10, 1 Cor. 4:20, 2 Cor. 12:9

LOVE
Source: Holman Christian Standard Bible

John 15:12-13: **This is My command: Love one another as I have loved you. No one has greater love than this, that someone would lay down his life for his friends.** Also read Romans 8:39.

REPENTANCE PRODUCES

FREEDOM
Source: English Standard Version

II Cor. 3:17 **"Now the Lord is the Spirit, and where the Spirit of the Lord is, there is freedom."** Also read Galatians 5:1 & 13-14, Eph. 3:12, Acts 13:38-39, Romans 6:22, 1 Peter 2:16, John 8:31-32

HOLINESS
Source: New International Version

II Tim. 1:9: **He has saved us and called us to a holy life— not because of anything we have done but because of his own purpose and grace. This grace was given us in Christ Jesus before the beginning of time.** Also read 1 Cor. 7:1, Heb. 12:14, 1 Peter 1:15-16, and Eph. 5:3

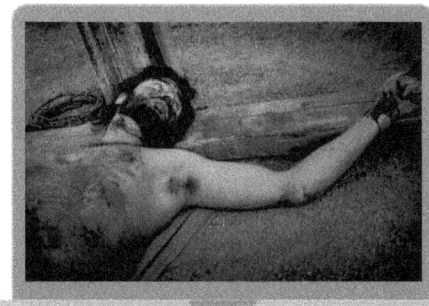

SELF CONTROL
Source: English Standard Version

1 Cor. 10:13: **No temptation has overtaken you that is not common to man. God is faithful, and he will not let you be tempted beyond your ability, but with the temptation he will also provide the way of escape, that you may be able to endure it.** Also read 2 Tim. 1:7, Prov. 16:32, Prov. 25:28, Titus 1:8, Romans 12:1-2

RIGHTEOUSNESS
Source: English Standard Version

Psalm 15:1-10: **O Lord, who shall sojourn in your tent? Who shall dwell on your holy hill? He who walks blamelessly and does what is right and speaks truth in his heart; who does not slander with his tongue and does no evil to his neighbor, nor takes up a reproach against his friend; in whose eyes a vile person is despised, but who honors those who fear the Lord; who swears to his own hurt and does not change; who does not put out his money at interest and does not take a bribe against the innocent. He who does these things shall never be moved.**

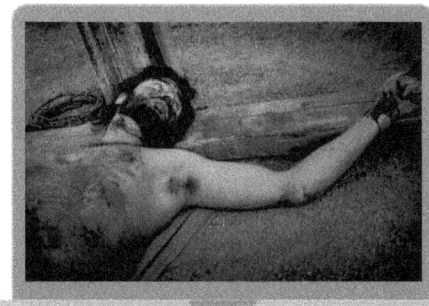

REPENTANCE PRODUCES

PEACE
Source: English Standard Version

John 14:27: **Peace I leave with you; my peace I give to you. Not as the world gives do I give to you. Let not your hearts be troubled, neither let them be afraid.** Also read Romans 5:1, Philippians 4:7, Isaiah 26:3, and Colossians 3:15.

SECURITY/PROTECTION
Source: New International Version

Nahum 1:7: **The Lord is good, a refuge in times of trouble. He cares for those who trust in him.** Also read 2 Cor. 4:8-9, 1 Cor. 10:13, 2 Thess. 3:3, Deut. 31:6, Isaiah 41:10, Psalm 12:5, Psalm 34:19, Psalm 46:1, Psalm 138:7, 2 Samuel 22:3-4, John 10:28, Psalm 23, Psalm 121, Psalm 91, Psalm 127:1

GOOD WORKS
Source: New International Version

Matt. 5:16: **In the same way, let your light shine before others, that they may see your good deeds and glorify your Father in heaven.** Also read Eph. 4:28, Exodus 17:12, Heb. 6:10, Luke 6:38, Gal. 6:2, Matt 5:42, Matt. 10:8, Philippians 2:4, Proverbs 3:27, Prov. 19:17, Prov. 22:9, Rom. 12:13, 1 John 4:19-20, Luke 12:33-34, Matt. 25:35-45, Luke 3:10-11, James 2:14-17, Luke 10:25-37(Good Samaritan), Proverbs 16:3

ETERNAL LIFE
Source: New International Version

John 3:16-17: **For God so loved the world that he gave his one and only Son, that whoever believes in him shall not perish but have eternal life. For God did not send his Son into the world to condemn the world, but to save the world through him.** Also read John 4:14, John 17:3, Matt. 7:13-14, Matt. 25:46, 1 John 5:13-14, Romans 10:8-10, Acts 16:31

PREPARATION

REPENTANCE

Repentance produces duplication in others: Romans 10:14-15: **How, then, can they call on the one they have not believed in? And how can they believe in the one of whom they have not heard? And how can they hear without someone preaching to them? And how can anyone preach unless they are sent?** As it is written: "How beautiful are the feet of those who bring good news!"(Isaiah 52:7). Also read 2 Tim. 2:2, 2 Tim. 3:16, and 1 Peter 3:21.

"Be careful not to do your 'acts of righteousness' in front of others, to be seen by them. If you do, you will have no reward from your Father in heaven." Matthew 6:1

PREPARATION

KEY TAKEAWAYS

- Evaluate your associations
- Exercise courage to say no
- Repent
- Your repentance produces a harvest
- Your change will be duplicated in others

We discussed how evil associations corrupt good morals. You must decide which connections, whether family or friends, will remain apart of your inner circle. Do they align with where God is taking you? The final decision is yours to make, so choose wisely. This will require you to exercise courage to say no to people, places and things that no longer serve where you're going. The question is: How bad do you want *change*?

Repent from bad behaviors and decisions that keep your soul from prospering. Don't stay anchored to old patterns and ways of thinking. Renew your mind daily with the Word of God.

Then your repentance will produce a harvest that includes a new heart, the presence of God's Spirit, power, love, freedom, holiness, self-control, righteousness, peace, protection, good works and eternal life.

PREPARATION

NOTES

PREPARATION

NOTES

SECTION 4: SPIRITUAL WEAPONS

"THE TRUTH *CAN* HURT, BUT IT CAN ALSO HEAL, REVEAL AND TRANSPORT YOU TO PLACES YOU ONLY DREAMED OF."

Lauraine White

WHAT IS TRUTH?

Philosophers have debated this topic for thousands of years and they remain divided on how to adequately describe what it is. Merriam Webster defines truth in three parts: the body of real things, events, and facts, such as a transcendent fundamental or spiritual reality; a judgment, proposition, or idea that is true or accepted as true; and the body of true statements and propositions.

When narrowed down to one element, it is considered to be a belief grounded in fact. Truth is absolute. It's not subjective or related to who's making an assessment on whether something is or is not true. It doesn't require our acceptance for it to be true. The truth is. Period.

ABSOLUTE TRUTH

The truth that is relevant to this masterclass is that Jesus is the Son of God, who left heaven, was born of a virgin, performed many miracles as signs of His deity, was scourged, beaten, then hung on a cross to die for us. But the story didn't end there. After Jesus's death, they buried him in a tomb and on the third day was risen. He walked the earth, after His resurrection for approximately 40 days, as evidence that He died and was brought back to life.

No other human being has ever done anything like that and never will. Jesus is the one and only Savior of the world because of what He did. He left evidence of His existence, death, burial, and resurrection.

It gets even better than that. On the 40th day after Jesus was resurrected, His disciples watched as He ascended back to heaven and was taken up in a cloud.

Jesus is still alive. Over 2000 years later, He's still as relevant today as He was back then. And as a show of good faith regarding our promised home in heaven, Jesus left His Spirit as a sort of down payment to ensure that nothing will keep us from our heavenly home.

SCRIPTURE REFERENCES

John 1:14
John 4:24
John 8:31-32
John 14:6
John 15:26
John 17:17
Ephesians 1:13-14
Proverbs 30:5
Ephesians 4:11-16
Philippians 4:8
1 Peter 1:23
James 1:18

45

THE WORD OF GOD

IT'S TRUTH SAVES US

The Truth that Jesus the Christ is God's Son.

The Truth that Jesus is God in the flesh that dwells among us.

The Truth that Jesus was born of the virgin Mary.

The Truth that Jesus is our Savior and Lord.

The Truth that Jesus was crushed for our iniquities, crucified, buried, resurrected for our freedom, and is alive forevermore.

The Truth that Jesus's shed blood is the atoning blood of the Lamb that purges us from our sin.

46

"THOSE WHO USE THE SWORD WILL DIE BY THE SWORD."

- MATTHEW 26:52

SPIRITUAL WEAPONS

TRUTH IS A WEAPON

The Truth transforms our mindset. It takes us from our ignorance to the understanding of who we are when we accept Christ's Truth that He is our Savior.

It exposes the deception of the enemy where our minds were conditioned to believe anything other than the truths that were mentioned on the previous pages.

When we marinate on these Truths, through consistent prayer, meditation, and study of the Word, allowing the Holy Spirit to penetrate our understanding of these truths, mind transformation takes place. Eph. 4:17-24; Romans 12:1-2

And do not be conformed to this world, but be transformed by the renewing of your mind, that you may prove what is that good and acceptable and perfect will of God. Romans 12:2

TRUTH AS A SPIRITUAL WEAPON

Truth then becomes a weapon through this transformation that occurs in our minds. "As a man thinks in his heart, so is he" Proverbs 23:7. This knowledge gives us strength to face any circumstance.

Knowing the Truth is essential to our salvation and would not have occurred except by the Supernatural and Divine empowerment of God Himself.

TRUTH REVEALED

God chose to reveal His Plan to man by supernatural means. Please read the following scriptures: Amos 3:6-8; 1 Corinthians 2:10; John 15:15; Revelations 10:7; Genesis 18:17; Jeremiah 23:22; Ezekiel 29:21; Daniel 2:47; Daniel 9:22-27; Psalm 25:14.

The person of the Holy Spirit is the "down payment" for the Promises of God, which seals the eternal "deal" for us. Read Ephesians 1:3-14.

THE HOLY SPIRIT

This diagram outlines how the Holy Spirit works and why He's essential to us living holy lives; thereby, sealing our understanding that our salvation is secure.

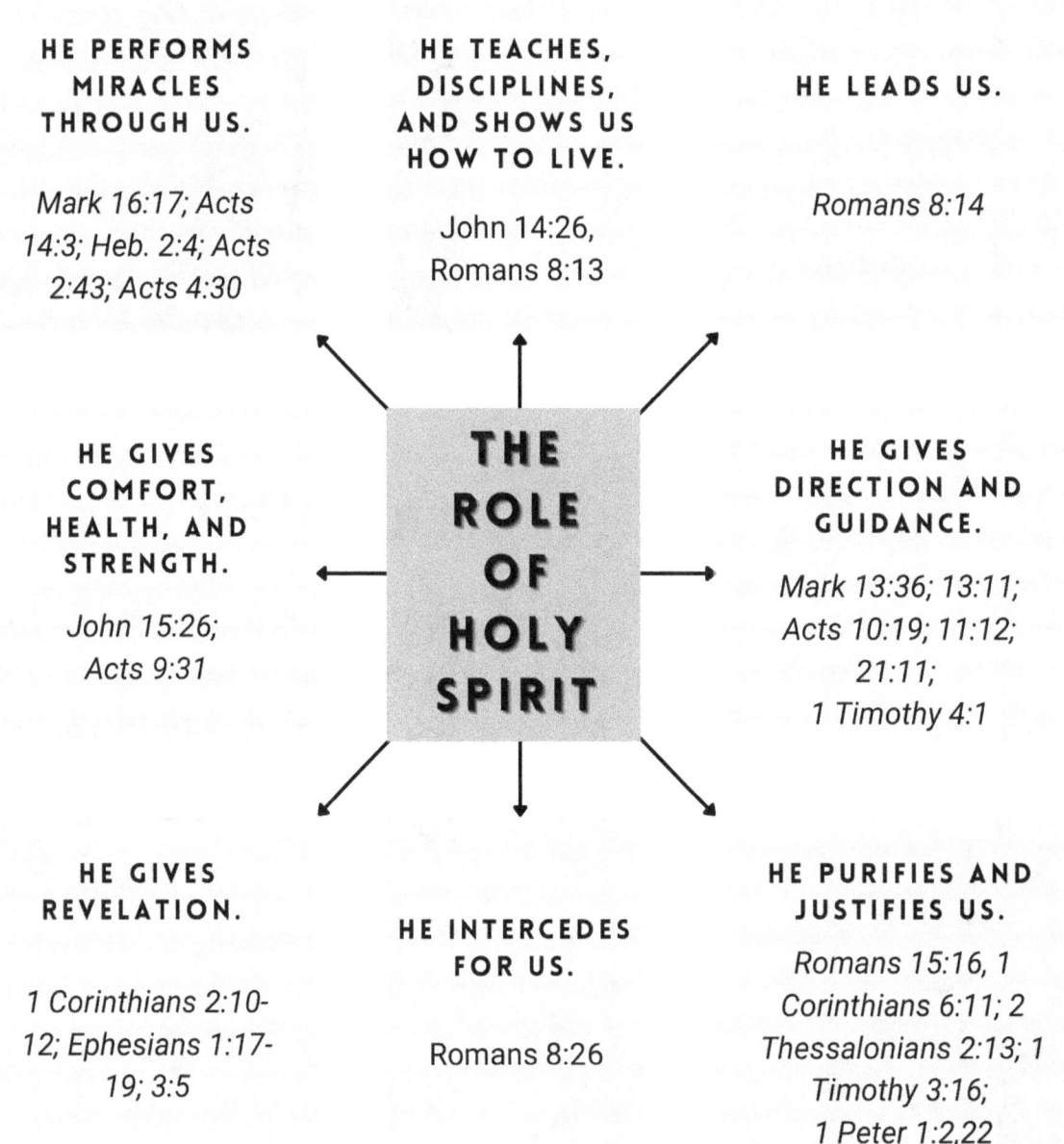

HE PERFORMS MIRACLES THROUGH US.

Mark 16:17; Acts 14:3; Heb. 2:4; Acts 2:43; Acts 4:30

HE TEACHES, DISCIPLINES, AND SHOWS US HOW TO LIVE.

John 14:26, Romans 8:13

HE LEADS US.

Romans 8:14

HE GIVES COMFORT, HEALTH, AND STRENGTH.

John 15:26; Acts 9:31

THE ROLE OF HOLY SPIRIT

HE GIVES DIRECTION AND GUIDANCE.

Mark 13:36; 13:11; Acts 10:19; 11:12; 21:11; 1 Timothy 4:1

HE GIVES REVELATION.

1 Corinthians 2:10-12; Ephesians 1:17-19; 3:5

HE INTERCEDES FOR US.

Romans 8:26

HE PURIFIES AND JUSTIFIES US.

Romans 15:16, 1 Corinthians 6:11; 2 Thessalonians 2:13; 1 Timothy 3:16; 1 Peter 1:2,22

This Truth of who the Holy Spirit is and His role in our salvation is a key to unlocking your understanding of spiritual warfare. We don't wage war like the world because Jesus has already defeated the enemy and won the war. We rest in Him and the strategies for overcoming that Holy Spirit deposits in us.

50

"WE ALL HAVE THE SAME DRILL SERGEANT. HIS NAME IS HOLY SPIRIT."

- LAURAINE WHITE

Holy Spirit

HE GIVES US GIFTS

1 Corinthians 12:4-11; Hebrews 2:4

- ☐ Word of wisdom
- ☐ Word of knowledge
- ☐ Faith
- ☐ Gifts of healing
- ☐ Working of miracles

- ☐ Prophecy
- ☐ Discerning of spirits
- ☐ Kinds of tongues
- ☐ Interpretation of tongues

WRITE YOUR THOUGHTS

_____ _____

_____ _____

_____ _____

_____ _____

_____ _____

_____ _____

_____ _____

_____ _____

TRUTH IS A WEAPON

THE TRUTH INFORMS US OF SATAN'S SCHEMES AND DECEPTIONS, EXPOSING ERROR IN OUR LIVES, AND GIVING WAY TO REPENTANCE.

So always seek Truth.

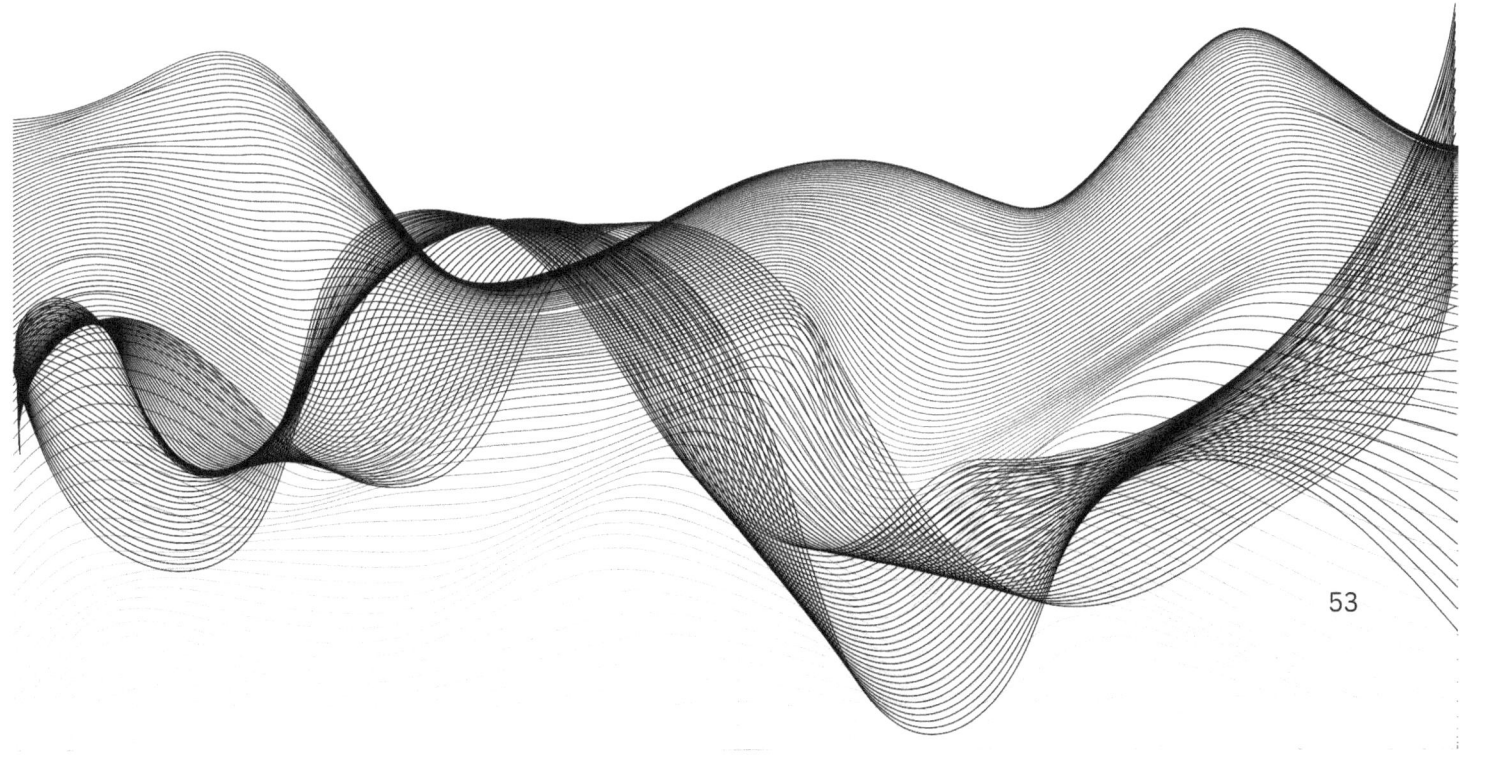

NOTES

NOTES

PRAISE & WORSHIP

Praise and worship, by definition, is to glorify God; to regard with great or extravagant respect, honor, or devotion. (Merriam-Webster.com)

"Come, let's shout praises to God, raise the roof for the Rock who saved us! Let's march into his presence singing praises, lifting the rafters with our hymns!" Psalm 95:1-3 MSG

As long as I can remember, I've been able to sing. So it was natural for me to join the choir and eventually the praise team. I love to sing all types of music: Whitney Houston, Aretha Franklin as well as other genres of music. But I especially love to sing praise and worship music. Something resonates in my soul when I sing about how good God has been to me.

What's the difference between praise and worship? Aren't they the same thing? Absolutely not, but they work hand in hand. I believe praise is an act given just because God exists. Praise is usually upbeat, joyous and lively. It opens the way for those in the congregation to enter into the Lord's presence. Psalm 100:4 says it best, "Enter into His gates with thanksgiving, and into His courts with praise. Be thankful to Him, and bless His name."

I can praise President Barak Obama for an outstanding presidency without knowing him personally. But when you know someone personally, such as when we know God one on one through our relationship with Jesus, we enter into a place of worship. Worship is our response to the relationship and the resulting benefits that come from the experience.

Worship is not manufactured. It's out of an abundant, grateful heart that worship is manifested. When this type of energy is generated and exerted by human beings in response to our great God, He responds. When your life becomes a demonstration of daily praise and worship, He makes your heart His home. His presence in you transports your spirit to heavenly realms where God is seated.

In Ephesians 2:6, it states, "And God raised us up with Christ and seated us with him in the heavenly realms in Christ Jesus." That means we have power when we are submitted to Christ.

56

SPIRITUAL WEAPONS

Whether you believe you have talent for singing or not, praise and worship is an essential element in spiritual warfare. In 2 Chronicles 20, the children of Israel found themselves up against a wall. They were surrounded by the armies of their enemies, who declared war on them. Upon hearing the news, Jehoshaphat, who was the king of Israel at that time, called for the entire kingdom to fast and pray. As the kingdom came together in Jerusalem, Jehoshaphat prayed to God in front of the entire assembly and began his prayer with praise and worship to God. He offered up praise and worship through his prayer.

As they were all gathered together, in unity, the Spirit of the Lord came on Jahaziel, a Levite, who gave the message that God would be with them as they went against their enemies. Upon hearing this, King Jehoshaphat bowed down and worshipped God and so did all of the people. They didn't murmur or complain. They worshipped and God responded.

After this encounter, the king appointed singers to go out ahead of the army, singing praises to God. The word says that at the moment they began singing, God caused the army of their enemies to start fighting each other. They didn't even have to fight. That's the power praise and worship has. And Satan knows this all too well, since he was the leader of praise and worship in heaven prior to being banished to hell. His goal is to keep you from it so that you never realize the power you have at your disposal.

KEY POINTS

Praise and worship is essential. It's not about talent. It's about gaining God's attention when we are in the midst of trials and troubles.

Whether you're currently in a battle, leaving one, or about to head into one, we need to be equipped to handle every circumstance that we must face. Praise and worship is incredible because it happens in response to what God has done for us and He is the one that rescues us when we do it. That's a part of what He meant when He said that He is "Alpha and Omega." He originates praise and worship in us because of what He's done for us and He completely annihilates our enemies when we praise and worship Him. It's the great circle that surrounds us as a benefit of knowing God. But we don't do it just for what God can do for us. We do it because He's worthy of the highest praise.

PRAISE & WORSHIP

1 THANKSGIVING

We enter the Lord's gates with thanksgiving and praise.
Psalm 100:4

2 PRAISE

We call your walls Salvation and your gates praise. Isaiah 60:18
Note: A gate gives access and entrance. Praise is "a gate" that
gives us access and entrance into the presence of God.

3 SACRIFICE

Offer to God a sacrifice of Praise. Jer. 17:26; 33: 11; Hebrews
13:15. This is worship that causes others to worship God with
you.

4 INSTRUMENTS

Praise God with Instruments. Psalm 150. Are you able to play an
instrument? Praise and worship by playing instruments for God's
enjoyment.

5 DANCE

Praise God with the Dance. **Psalm 149:3; 150:4.** "You have
turned my mourning into joyful dancing." (Psalm 30:11 NLT)

6 CLAPPING HANDS

Clapping hands is an act of praise. Psalm 47: 1.

7 LIFTING HOLY HANDS

God inhabits the praises of His People. Psalm 22:3

PRAISE & WORSHIP

8 PURE HEART

Praise is not a tool for manipulation but comes from a pure heart toward God. Deut. 10:21; Jer. 17:14

9 BEING AUTHENTIC

Thankfulness and gratitude result in authentic praise and worship. 2 Corinthians 4:15; 2 Chronicles 5:13; Jeremiah 30:19; Psalm 9; 2 Samuel 22

10 LIFESTYLE

Lifestyle of praise and worship produces consistent answered prayers. Isaiah 38:18-20; Deuteronomy 6:7; 11:19; Psalm 78:4-5; 115:16-18; 118:17; 119:175; 145:4; 146:2; Ecclesiastes 9:10; John 9:4

11 BRINGS HEALING

Praise brings healing. Psalm 43:5; Acts 2:47 compared with Acts 3:8,9.

12 BRINGS THE GLORY OF GOD AND FIRE

II Chron. 5; 7: 1-3. After praise, worship and dedication of the Temple, fire flashed down from Heaven. The fire is a type of the Holy Spirit, and the temple is a type of temple not made by hands.

13 BRINGS DELIVERANCE

Praise brings deliverance. Acts 16:25, 26. While Paul and Silas were praying and singing from prison, an earthquake shook the foundation of the prison until all chains fell off all prisoners.

PRAISE & WORSHIP

14 BRINGS VICTORY AT JERICHO

Jericho fell at the sound of the trumpets after 7 days of the Israelites marching around the walls of the city. Joshua 6 (also II Chron. 7:6).

15 DEFEATED THE MIDIANITES

God told Gideon to reduce the army down to only 300 soldiers to fight against 135,000 men of Midian. God delivered victory to them because of *obedience*. Judges 7 (also II Chron. 7:6).

16 DEFEATED AMMON AND MOAB

Singing defeated Ammon and Moab. Remember that Judah was doing the singing. (Moab and Ammon were the incestuous sons of Lot.) II Chron. 20:22.

17 RESCUES US

"Gone up" used in the KJV refers to God ascending His throne to render judgment against our enemies. This may well have been a type of battle cry. Ps. 47:5-7.

18 BRINGS TRIUMPH

There is a triumph in praise. Ps. 106:47. God causes us to overcame every device of the enemy. He always causes us to win.

19 GIVES US BINDING POWER

Praise binds the kings and the nobles. These nobles are Satan's hosts. Ps. 149:6-9. The believer has binding power. (Matt. 12:29; 16: 19; 18: 18). With this the psalmist agrees. "This honor have all his saints."

NOTES

NOTES

PRAYER

Read chapter 8: The Lighthouse in "Bulletproof" companion book.

As a young woman, I was quite arrogant and self assured until life bit me, sucker punching me until my life hit a brick wall and began rolling down hills of empty promises and unfulfilled dreams. I was depressed, broken and ashamed of what I had become but I didn't know how to get up out of the wreckage and fix my life.

As time passed, life got tougher. But when times get tough, the tough get going, right? Wrong. I wallowed in my broken state of mind. My marriage was a wreck and my children suffered because I couldn't see a way out. I was just going through the motions of living.

Where was God in all of this mess that I found myself in? He was there. He was speaking. Life was just louder.

Then I found prayer. It began to soothe my soul as I started seeing changes emerge that I had asked for while praying. I was on to something.

Prayer changed my life. Through my prayers, I developed an unshakeable relationship with Jesus. I also gained an authority that caused demons to flee, sicknesses to be eradicated--not just in others but also in my own body, and weather patterns to change.

PUSH
(PRAY UNTIL SOMETHING HAPPENS)

How did I gain this authority, you may ask? I gained it by trusting that God can do anything but fail. When life hurled its massacre attempts at me, I turned to the Rock, my fortress, who is Jesus, the Christ. I confessed to Him that I was a sinner in need of His saving grace and that I needed Him to help me. And He did. Ever single time, He came through for me.

Every time that Jesus came to rescue me, I got a little more confidence in Him. Until one day, the demons working against me were so bold that they made my house their home.

The fight became personal. I had a lot at stake. They were operating through my loved ones. Every time that I saw my husband, I could physically see demonic spirits. Church people almost convinced me that I was crazy, except I knew that my husband and children had accepted Jesus as their Lord and Savior but demons were controlling them.

Without anyone to help me, I turned to the only source I had. Prayer. I prayed for God to send help and He did. Through that help, I learned the art of spiritual warfare and the skill of waiting on God. It's a skill because while you wait, there are things that you must do to prepare for the moment that God answers.

No matter whether you depend on Jesus or not, trouble is going to find you because it is a human dilemma that we all have to go through. The question for you is do you want to take a chance at going through life without His help or would you prefer to have a trusted friend walk along side you as you navigate your way out?

"YOUR LIFE MATTERS AND EVERY STEP YOU TAKE HAS BEEN ORDERED BY GOD!"

AUTHORITY

When I was a child, I remember when then President Jimmy Carter appointed Andrew Young to be an Ambassador to the United Nations. It was a big deal. He was from my hometown, Atlanta, GA and he was an African American. With this appointment came much authority to him and it was a great accomplishment to be the first of slave descent to hold such a position of authority.

The authority that we have in Christ is like that mentioned in Mark 13:34, "For the Son of man is as a man taking a far journey, who left his house, and gave authority to his servants, and to every man his work, and commanded the porter to watch."

We are God's ambassadors. An ambassador is an official envoy; especially a diplomatic agent of the highest rank accredited to a foreign government or sovereign as the resident representative of his or her own government or sovereign or appointed for a special and often temporary diplomatic assignment. (As defined by Merriam-Webster.com)

Whether you sing in the choir, teach a bible study or sit in the pew, this is the assignment of every believer—not just church leadership. If you believe in Jesus, you are His ambassador.

AUTHORITY

What is the job of an ambassador? According to the Vienna Convention on Diplomatic Relations of 1961, of which is still in effect, an ambassador is of the highest position who represents the Head of state with full authority to represent its home government. The position of ambassador is confirmed by the governing body of its country and their authority is based on the region for which they were selected.

But what does that mean for you and me? It means that we are now ministers of reconciliation. 2 Corinthians 5:18-21 states, "All this is from God, who through Christ reconciled us to himself and gave us the ministry of reconciliation; that is, in Christ God was reconciling the world to himself, not counting their trespasses against them, and entrusting to us the message of reconciliation. Therefore, we are ambassadors for Christ, God making his appeal through us. We implore you on behalf of Christ, be reconciled to God. For our sake he made him to be sin who knew no sin, so that in him we might become the righteousness of God.

In essence, we become His witnesses in the earth. We proclaim the Good News of the Gospel and the atoning Blood of Jesus that takes away the sins of the world.

But when we come in the name of Jesus with this message of reconciliation, demons get angry and rear their heads. They don't want the message of Jesus coming to save the world to reach those that need it the most. Therefore, that's the reason for the spiritual warfare. But rest assured, Jesus already overcame these forces when He got up out of the grave and He lives forevermore.

So don't be afraid of the walls of water that form all around you as God brings you into the place of promise. Trust Him. Jesus is in control and will never leave you--no matter what comes or goes.

That's why we must learn to pray without ceasing. It's our Central Command Station and all tactical strategies are deployed through prayer.

AMBASSADOR

It's important that you understand who you are because you confess Jesus as your Savior. Supernatural authority has been given but it's not until you fully understand your role that you can exercise this level of authority.

STEP ONE

THE CHURCH

The Church is the Embassy of God. The place of refuge for the Sovereign subjects or ambassadors. This is to be a safe place for those who rest in Christ.

STEP TWO

DELEGATED AUTHORITY

We, as ambassadors of Christ, have delegated authority. This means that the King has given us the right to bind and loose on earth as we are instructed by the Spirit of God.

STEP THREE

SUPREME POWER

Delegated Authority has the same rights and power of the Supreme Original. This means the same power that resurrected Jesus from the grave is working in us.

AUTHORITY

The following are exercises for you to read scripture and allow the Holy Spirit to give you insight on the implementation strategy that has been given to you individually. Only He knows the plans that He has for you. Stay sensitive to the Spirit as He leads you.

ASK YOURSELF...

WRITE YOUR ANSWERS HERE....

Read Ephesians 2:4-10. What does it mean for us to be seated together in heavenly places in Christ Jesus?

Read Ephesians 1:3-23. What does it mean when it states that all things are under Christ's feet?

Read James 4:7. How do we submit our will to line up with the Will of God and not the other way around?

STRATEGIES FOR BATTLE

K.C.A.P. - Knowledge, Confidence, Assurance and Power are elements that are strapped around you like armor.

1

KNOWLEDGE

Know your enemy. It's not people. It's Satan and his army of demons. So, don't fight with people. In Matthew 5:43-44, Jesus said to love your enemies because He knows the enemies' strategies against us are meant to confuse who's really working..

2

CONFIDENCE

Know that the battle is already won. Jesus did that at Calvary and by His resurrection. That's why we're considered ambassadors. We're enforcers more than soldiers fighting our enemies. The strategy is to pray God's Word and He will watch over it to perform it. Trust Him.

3

ASSURANCE

Put your faith to the test. According to Deuteronomy 20:1-4, when you go into battle, be assured that God is with you and that He's never lost a battle.

4

POWER

Your thoughts and words have power so use them wisely. Proverbs 18:21 states, "Life and death are in the power of the tongue, and those who love it will eat its fruit." (HCSB Version)

AUTHORITY IN PRAYER

Know your rights as a believer and ambassador, and then use it. "As a man thinketh in his heart, so is he," and "believe and you will receive."
1 Corinthians 12:1-11; Proverbs 23:7; Matthew 21:22

- [ ] Word of wisdom

- [ ] Word of knowledge

- [ ] Faith

- [ ] Gifts of healing

- [ ] Miracles

- [ ] Prophecy

- [ ] Distinguishing between spirits

- [ ] Tongues

- [ ] Interpretation of tongues

ADMINISTER AUTHORITY

Read chapter 10: The Chase in "Bulletproof" companion book.

Have you ever noticed how when you come into a dark room then turn on the overhead light, how darkness flees, until dark shadows from the objects in the room are all the darkness that remains? Close your eyes. Now picture it.

That's how Satan works. As long as he remains in dark rooms, he feels at home to do his dirty work. But when the light comes, he flees. All that he can do when the light appears is hide behind objects or people as life goes. So don't let the shadows of Satan frighten you or keep you from doing what you were born to do. Those shadows are afraid of the light shining through you.

The dark room represents the evil things of this world that you allow your mind to focus on. That encompasses how you use your senses. It's what you see, hear, absorb, smell, and taste that matters. It influences who you become. If you focus only on eating food, you will become overweight. If you focus on scientific research, you will become a scientist. It's important that when it comes to matters of your spirit, that you guard what your senses take in because it will determine who rules your decisions. If you focus too much on any one thing, your soul and spirit become out of balance.

So it's important that once you receive Jesus as your Savior that you spend time with the Holy Spirit. He will lead you to understand the process to take to clean out your soul. Who from your past or your present do you need to forgive? What are you holding on to that will keep you from where God wants to take you? Take time to delve into this. You will be surprised at how it will not just free your mind but it will change your countenance. It also increases your authority when you pray.

You can't fully decree a thing and it be established when your soul is so full of unforgiveness. It interrupts the flow of God. So work on you. Make it a priority because you matter and what God has for you matters.

What you are coming into is not by natural means. It's supernatural. It's Spirit and Light. You can't fully appreciate the nature of it all until you do the work necessary to become ready to be used by God in ways that He intends.

Satan wants to keep you trapped and confused. He wants you to believe lies instead of the Truth because he's afraid that when you do this work, you will become a force he has to reckon with.

HIGHLIGHTS

"Through him all things were made; without him nothing was made that has been made. In him was life, and that life was the light of all mankind. **The light shines in the darkness, and the darkness has not overcome it.**" John 1:3-5 NIV

There's safety in the light. For when the light comes, darkness has to flee. So let your light shine because light belongs in darkness. Let the Holy Spirit lead you to do the work necessary to prepare you for the assignments ahead of you. Don't allow the past to short circuit the power of your witness. You are God's workmanship, a masterpiece formed in God's hand to do great and mighty works.

ADMINISTER AUTHORITY

*"And God said, Let us make man in our image, after our likeness: and **let them have dominion** over the fish of the sea, and over the fowl of the air, and over the cattle, and over all the earth, and over every creeping thing that creepeth upon the earth."*
Genesis 1:26

Decree & Declare God's Will from the place of victory. *Job 22:27-29: "You will pray to Him, and He will hear you; and you will pay your vows. You will also decree a thing, and it will be established for you; and light will shine on your ways. When you are cast down, you will speak with confidence, and the humble person He will save. Read: MARK 16:14-20; MATTHEW 7:22; LUKE 10:17; ACTS 19:13; MATTHEW 12:27*

73

ADMINISTER AUTHORITY

In prayer, we make declarations or decrees because of our position as ambassadors of Christ. This means we demand God's will be done on earth, as it is in heaven.

QUESTIONS:

WRITE YOUR ANSWERS HERE...

Read Ephesians 6:10-12. **Explain what it means here to be strong.** "Finally, my brethren, be strong in the Lord, and in the power of his might. Put on the whole armor of God, that ye may be able to stand against the wiles of the devil. For we wrestle not against flesh and blood, but against principalities, against powers, against the rulers of the darkness of this world, against spiritual wickedness in high places."

Read Matthew 7:7. **How does this scripture relate to being certain of God's Promises?** "Ask, and it will be given to you; seek, and you will find; knock, and it will be opened to you."

Read Isaiah 40:30. **What comes to mind when you hear the statement "wait on God?" Do you feel this is your season to wait on God? Are you willing to wait?** But those who wait on the Lord shall renew their strength; They shall mount up with wings like eagles, They shall run and not be weary, They shall walk and not faint.

74

"Be still, and know that I am God;
I will be exalted among the nations,
I will be exalted in the earth!"

Psalm 46:10

NOTES

NOTES

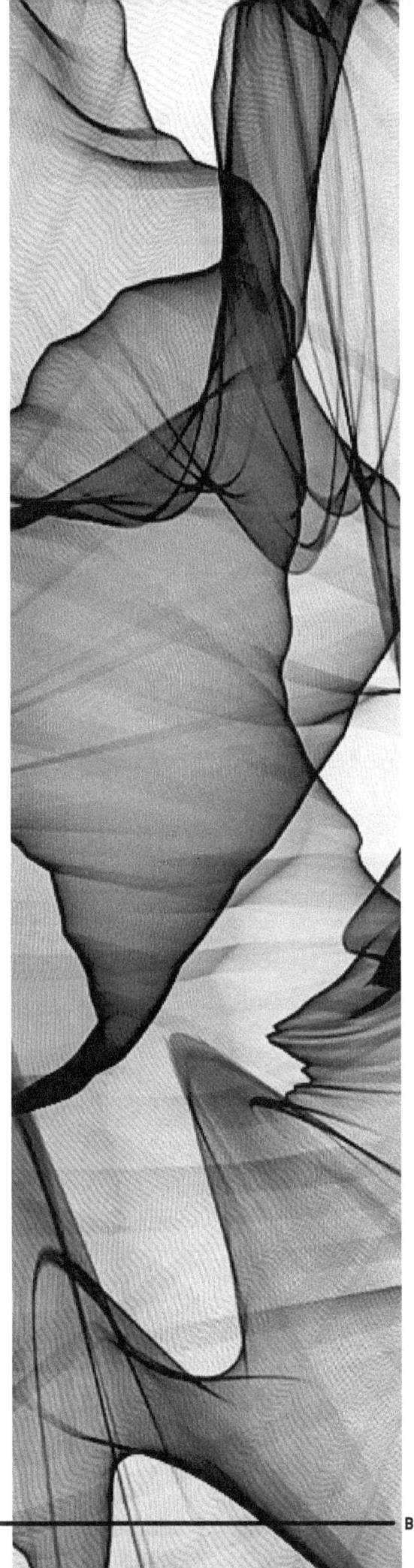

ABIDE

ABIDE

To endure without yielding; to bear patiently; withstand; to wait for; to accept without objection. (Merriam-Webster.com)

Read chapter 7: View from the Valley in "Bulletproof" companion book.

"Abide in me, and I in you. As the branch cannot bear fruit by itself, unless it abides in the vine, neither can you, unless you abide in me." John 15:4

The word wait appears in the King James Version of the Holy Bible 154 times between the Old and New Testaments. Waiting is difficult. Everyone in our world is absorbed with being in a hurry. We have fast food; drive through coffee; we order products online for it to be shipped overnight. We can't stand waiting. But waiting is a necessary part of life.

With God, you must get comfortable with waiting. But while you wait, there are things that you need to do to prepare for what's coming next. Waiting is not a sedentary exercise. Waiting involves sharpening your skills.

Many times, the process of waiting is for us. Maybe the wait is for us to shape up. It could be that there are things that we need to purge from so that we are ready for God to work through us. It's God's process of refining us. The wait is to make you, not to break you. Submit to the process and you will be glad you did.

Once, when I moved back to Atlanta, I moved to an apartment intown. It was very convenient to the office but I had been away from Atlanta for almost four years. I didn't realize how the street that I was moving to had become pretty rough.

The day after I moved in, I noticed that there were some very strange things going on in the apartment below me. There were maybe five or six women living together with a guy.

There were activities going on in that unit all night long. People were coming and going. They were slamming the door every hour. I couldn't sleep with all the commotion.

One Sunday afternoon, the first week that I was there, this guy came into their unit screaming, yelling, and slamming doors. The first thought that I had was I need to report them to the management office. Then the Holy Spirit said, "no, don't report them. Pray for them."

79

Pray for them? I was stunned. The Spirit of God reminded me of a Word that He gave me several years before where He spoke these words: "I am bringing redemption in dark places." The Spirit of God began to show me that this young man's relative, maybe a grandmother prayed his entire life for God to save him and that he sent me to pray and decree the turnaround.

Here I was. Abiding. Waiting for the release of what God promised me but He asked me to participate with Him to finish the work started by someone else. It seemed beyond me. But God moved on me to understand that abiding in Him means that as I remain in Him, He needs me to do the work that He sent me to do.

I thought it was all about me but I'm just a vessel that He can use. There's nothing special about a vessel. You fill it up to water the flowers or you use it to make sweet tea. The vessel is the pass through. Its the water that waters the flowers or the people enjoying the freshly made sweet tea that matters. So get out of yourself. Don't get tripped up because of your ego. Let it go.

I lived in that apartment nine months and for nine months, I prayed earnestly over that entire household including the entire street that had become overrun with strip clubs. The month before I moved out, each intersection on both sides of the complex experienced a major fire that shut down traffic in all directions. I believe those fires represent God answering the prayers of someone that submitted to the process of abiding in Him. This is the type of fruit that comes from abiding or remaining in Jesus, like the branch remaining in the vine.

KEY POINTS

Waiting does not mean being stagnant. You're still moving in the right direction. Remain steadfast, unmovable and unshakeable in Jesus and His promises. Then watch how He develops the character in you that helps change the world.

ABIDE

As you learn to abide, it's important to express your heart to God. Read the following scriptures: 1 Thess. 5:18, Col. 3:17, Col. 4:2, John 14:1 The following are examples from the Bible of men that expressed their concerns to God and how they were answered.

JACOB WRESTLED WITH GOD. READ GENESIS 32:22-32

JOSEPH WEPT AT SEEING HIS BROTHERS. READ GENESIS 42:24; 43:30-31

ELIJAH CRIED OUT TO GOD FOR THE SON OF THE ZAREPHATH WOMAN. READ 1 KINGS 17:20

ELIJAH, WHILE HIDDEN IN A CAVE, CRIED OUT FOR HELP. READ 1 KINGS 19:1-18

MOSES COMPLAINED TO GOD. READ EXODUS 5:22 THROUGH 6:13, NUMBERS 11:10-15

JONAH DIDN'T WANT GOD TO SAVE NINEVEH AND COMPLAINED TO HIM. READ JONAH 2

SAMSON ASKED TO DIE WITH THE PHILISTINES. READ JUDGES 16:23-31

JESUS ASKED TO BE EXCUSED FROM HIS ASSIGNMENT. READ MATT. 26:36-46

ABIDING IN PRAYER

Abiding in prayer involves your position. Here are
examples of positions to use when praying.

WALK

Joshua 6:1-5

KNEEL

Psalm 95:6, Daniel 6:10, I Kings 8:54,
2 Chron. 6:13, Phil. 2:9-11

LIE PROSTRATE

Genesis 17:1-22, Numbers 20:2-6, Joshua
7:1-6, Neh. 8:6, Matt. 26:39, Luke 5:12,
Revelation 1:17

LIFTED HANDS

Exodus 9:27–29, Psalm 141:2,
1 Timothy 2:8

SILENCE

Psalm 46:10, 1 Sam. 1:13

BIRTHING POSITION

1 Kings 18:41-46

ABIDING IN PRAYER

STEP ONE

MAKE TIME FOR GOD

James 4:8, John 15:5, Psalm 46:10: Psalm 131:2, Philippians 4:7, Romans 8:6, Isaiah 26:3

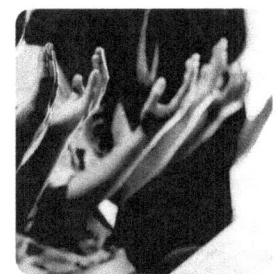

STEP TWO

USE THE WORD OF GOD

But you're not limited to it. The Spirit of God will give you what you need. Joshua 1:8, Psalm 119:147-148

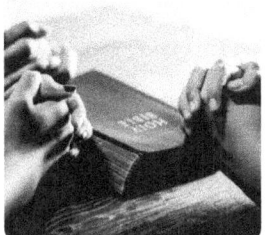

STEP THREE

LISTEN

James 1:19-22, Luke 10:39, Luke 11:28, 1 John 4:1, 1John 5:14-15, Jeremiah 29:12, Psalm 5:3, John 10:27, Matt. 7:24-27, 1 Samuel 3:9-10

STEP FOUR

WAIT FOR GOD'S ANSWER

Psalm 27:14, Psalm 37:7, Psalm 123:2, Jeremiah 14:22, Psalm 25:5, Psalm 5:3, Psalm 33:20, Psalm 130:5, Isaiah 51:5, Micah 7:7, Lamentations 3:24-26, Rev. 6:9-11, Gen. 49:18, Psalm 39:7

STEP FIVE

ENCOURAGE EACH OTHER

Prayer is not just a solitary practice. It's done in community as well. 1 Thess. 5:11

NOTES

NOTES

ARMED

Read chapter 2: Armed and Dangerous in "Bulletproof" companion book.

"Finally, my brethren, be strong in the Lord, and in the power of his might. Put on the whole armor of God, that ye may be able to stand against the wiles of the devil. For we wrestle not against flesh and blood, but against principalities, against powers, against the rulers of the darkness of this world, against spiritual wickedness in high places."
Ephesians 6:10-12

It all started with a dream. I was sitting in a car in a nice area of town. I was waiting on someone. While sitting in the driver's seat, I heard gun shots in the distance and I began to look around for whomever it was that I was waiting on. But no one showed up.

Then the gun shots grew louder and came closer to where I was. So I tried to hide. I slid down in the driver's seat because I didn't know what else to do. Then the gun shots were directed at me. One gunmen after another stood at the car that I was in until it was completely surrounded. They lit into the car. With high powered guns, they unloaded one round after another round directly at the car that I was in.

There was smoke everywhere and I was so afraid. The smell of the gun smoke took my breath away but the intensity with which they unleashed their anger toward me was unnerving.

Why were they after me? What did I do to cause all these gunmen to want me dead? What caused them to be consumed with killing me?

86

After the gun shots stopped and the gunmen left the area where I was, people began coming over to the car, looking in, assuming that I was dead. I wasn't dead. I was alive. I got up from my hiding place trying to get their attention to let them know that I survived. But no one paid attention to me. It was as if I were invisible.

Then I saw with my peripheral vision, a white wing flapping on the outside of the car. What was that? I had to see what that was. I got out of the car, without opening the car door and saw the most amazing sight. There were angels completely surrounding the car that I had been in. They were side by side with one wing overlapping another wing until the entire car was covered with angels. They didn't look at me or say a word. They looked straight ahead. They were there to perform God's Word that I had been praying and fasting for. They were there all along. I was just unaware of their presence.

I was armed and dangerous. I just didn't know it at the time. Through my faith, prayers and fasting, I had become enemy number one to Satan and his imps. You see most of 2006 and 2007, I fasted more than I ate. I didn't know what was going on in the spirit realm but there was so much uneasiness that I felt the need to fast. That urgency to fast coupled with my faith that God would answer made me a target. But when the enemy comes in like a flood, it's the Spirit of Almighty God that puts Satan in his place--the pit of hell is where he belongs. I was trying in my own strength to make something happen, but God was the only one that could deliver me.

That's what I'm here today to share with you. How to become equipped for the battles that are up ahead for you. You don't have to fear it. Just prepare for it.

"PUT ON THE WHOLE ARMOR OF GOD SO THAT YOU ARE EQUIPPED FOR EVERY CIRCUMSTANCE"

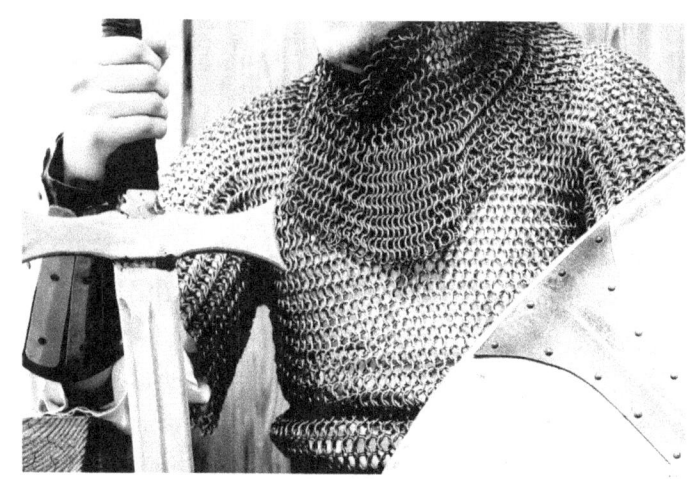

87

ARMED

BELT OF TRUTH

The belt of truth holds everything together. Jesus said, "I am the Way, the Truth, and the Life. No one comes to the Father, except through me." (John 14:6).Jesus called the Holy Spirit the "Spirit of Truth." (John 16:13) Jesus prayed for God to sanctify us by the Truth of His Word. (John 17:17) As we get everything that is untruthful out of our lives, we become more like Jesus. Without Him, we are unclothed and unprotected during battle.

BREASTPLATE OF RIGHTEOUSNESS

The breastplate of righteousness protects our hearts. "This righteousness is given through faith in Jesus Christ to all who believe." (Romans 3:22). Jesus makes us a new person created to desire Godly things. (Ephesians 4:22-24) But it's His righteousness, given to us (2 Corinthians 5:21), that we trust in, not our own.

THE SHIELD OF FAITH

The shield of faith is our trust in the promises of Jesus. Focusing on God's faithfulness can block accusations, doubts, and temptations that attack us. (Ephesians 6:16)

THE HELMET OF SALVATION

The helmet of salvation protects our thoughts. Our enemy falsely accuses and lies to us. "But let us who live in the light be clearheaded, protected by the armor of faith and love, and wearing as our helmet the confidence of our salvation" (1 Thessalonians 5:8)

THE SHOES OF THE GOSPEL

This represents the readiness given by the Gospel. It's important to know the truth of Jesus well enough to explain it to others. That makes your feet beautiful! "How beautiful on the mountains are the feet of the messenger who brings good news, the good news of peace and salvation, the goodness that God reigns!" (Isaiah 52:7).

THE SWORD OF THE SPIRIT

The sword of the spirit is the Word of God and our most powerful weapon of attack. We must become skilled in using it strategically.

NOTES

NOTES

FASTING AND PRAYING

"THE SUPREME ART OF WAR IS TO SUBDUE THE ENEMY WITHOUT FIGHTING."

- SUN TZU

FASTING AND PRAYING

MY STORY

It was September 2001, and we had just moved into what we thought would be our forever dream house. Little did I know that I was running right into a season of suffering, struggles, and hardships.

By all indications, I was at the top of my game. I had a successful daycare center, real estate sales practice, and I was Vice President of a local bank, but my personal life was running on life support.

What in the world happened? Demons happened. They moved into our house when we moved in. Satan got in bed with me every night disguised as my husband. I didn't know if I were coming or going, most of that time.

I became a prisoner in my own home. The closer I drew to God, the more intense the fight became at home. I felt like I was in the boxing ring of life, and I was swinging with everything I had.

But God sent an angel to help me. She taught me how to pray effectively and what it means to fast. As a result, I witnessed demons leave my husband, as they floated out of the window.

Read chapter 5: Target in "Bulletproof" companion book.

"For though we live in the world, we do not wage war as the world does. The weapons we fight with are not the weapons of the world. On the contrary, they have divine power to demolish strongholds. We demolish arguments and every pretension that sets itself up against the knowledge of God, and we take captive every thought to make it obedient to Christ." 2 Corinthians 10:3-5 NIV

"FASTING IS NOT FOR GOD. IT'S FOR YOU"

- LAURAINE WHITE

"How bad do you want it?" That's the question that I asked myself as I considered this idea of fasting and praying.

I was knocking down the door of 40 years old, at the time and it was as if my life hit a brick wall. So, *my soul* was asking, "How important is it to you that they be set free?" I loved my family dearly and I wanted them set free but what was it going to cost me to obtain the anointing that was necessary for their freedom?

It cost me everything. After experiencing the exorcism that happened in my home, I went on a quest to discover more about who I am in Christ and what power He has given us. I had to know more. I could no longer sit in silence, waiting in the balance for someone else to come save me.

If Jesus came to give me power to tread upon serpents, I wanted to know how to demonstrate it. The biblical stories written on those pages had to come to life for me. I would no longer accept just reading a good story about God's deliverance. I wanted to experience it, first hand.

But it seemed as if everywhere I went, they were selling church, not Jesus and I was over the good sermons from people that had no real experience with God. You know what I mean? It was like when we were children, just playing "church." But I'm no longer a child. I'm in search of a God who can save me.

Save me from what? The troubles of this life that no one prepares you for. Do you know what I mean? There's no manual for living. It's an on-the-job experience. Therefore, you need a coach, not a manual.

That Coach that we're all seeking is none other than the Holy Spirit. God's Master plan was intentional. With us in mind, God planned for Jesus to die, be resurrected and leave His Spirit for us to have someone live with us daily to show us how to live.

IF NOT NOW, WHEN?

Without the Holy Spirit, it's impossible for us to be totally free. And it's unattainable for us to live victoriously over an enemy that exists to cause troubles in our lives if we don't have the Holy Spirit.

No matter whether you choose to serve God or not, and as long as you're on this side of life, you will have adversities. You can't get around it. It's a guarantee. There are few things in life that are certain and they are: you will die, pay taxes and experience some form of struggle or hardship, no matter what your socio-economic status.

We're all connected together in this world and we need each other to survive. No one is an island, although, much of society today is isolated. And when you isolate yourself, your problems appear too big to handle.

Someone once said, "Life begins at the end of your comfort zone." So it's okay if you are sort of afraid to venture out into this new journey of discovery. If it doesn't frighten you a little, you wouldn't

be human. That's why you need to give your life, fully, to Jesus and submit to the leading of the Holy Spirit. Your Highest and best life can only be found in Him.

A part of that life surrounds fasting and praying. In the days and months ahead, we will examine this further in the following pages. As we do, I'm asking you to put some of what you've learned here into practice. Try going on a fast for a 24-hour period of time with no food--only water or tea combined with focused prayers.

I'm asking you what I asked of myself: How bad do you want it? If you're really okay with the status quo, that's cool. We're not here to push you to do something that you're not ready for. But if you have come to the place where you are sick and tired of being sick and tired and you've tried everything else, I suggest that you try Jesus through fasting and praying. Come with us as we go through this process of finding your power.

95

FASTING & PRAYING

What is fasting? It is not eating or only eating certain kinds of foods for a specific period of time in order to make prayer your priority.

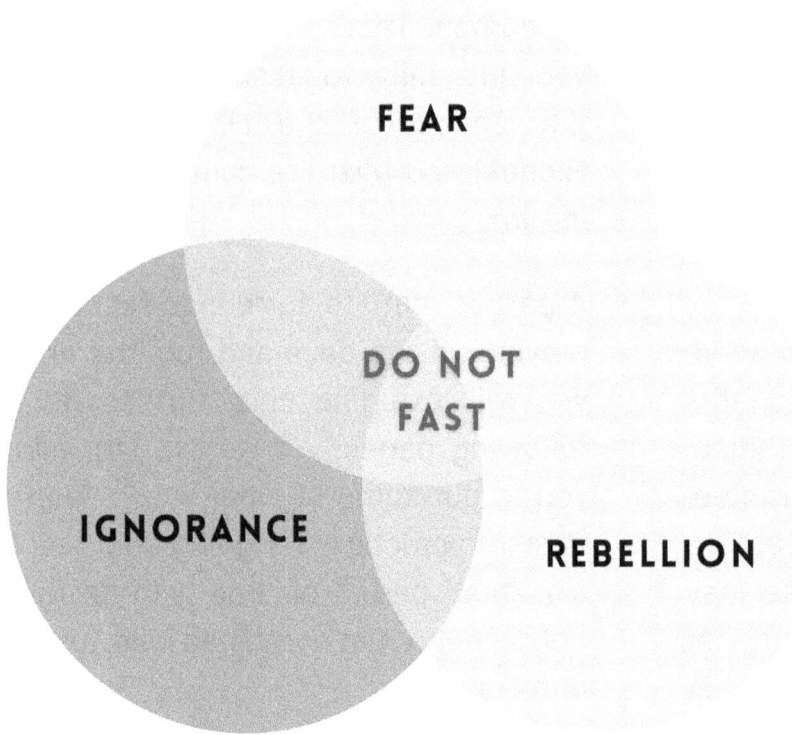

FEAR

You're afraid of what people may think. You're afraid of how it will make you feel to go without food.

IGNORANCE

Maybe you've never heard of this practice. No one has ever mentioned it to you.

REBELLION

This is like playing God as if He's a slot machine. There's no jackpot so you give up on God.

Here are some reasons why some people do not fast and pray. What are your reasons?

Fasting and praying is a good time to be transparent with yourself and God about who you are, who you want to become, and what God desires for you. It's a two-way form of communicating with God. You speak to Him and He speaks to you. You, reaching out to God in an uncomfortable way for you, shows Him how much you really need Him. It's also a time to renew your soul. Giving up some things for a short period of time can positively change some habits. Science says that if you do something for 21 days, it becomes a habit. Think about that. You're here because you want change.

WHAT PRAYER & FASTING IS NOT:

ONE

A BADGE OF HONOR

It makes you appear "holier than thou." – Read Luke 18:9-14 The Parable of the Pharisee and the Tax Collector

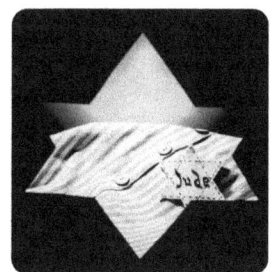

TWO

NOT A WEIGHT LOSS PROGRAM

Although you may lose weight while fasting and praying, that is not the goal. The goal is to draw closer to God so that you are able to petition the Throne of God for the answers you seek.

THREE

A WAY TO IMPRESS GOD

God is not impressed by outward shows of affection. He looks at the heart and judges what you do based on your motives. God is drawn to a broken and contrite heart.

FOUR

TO EARN AN ANSWER FROM GOD

Fasting and praying, from God's perspective, is about spending quality time with you. When you show genuine love and gratitude, God responds to your requests without hesitation, but He is not a sugar daddy that can be easily manipulated as man can be.

FIVE

FOR BOASTING

Some people want to look religious and they go around announcing when they are fasting. That's boasting and God is not pleased with that behavior. Jesus said do it in secret and what is done in secret, God will reward openly. Read Matthew 6:16-18

97

WHY SHOULD WE FAST?

JESUS EXPECTS US TO.

ONE

Read Matthew 6:16-18. "But when you fast, put oil on your head and wash your face, so that it will not be obvious to others that you are fasting, but only to your Father, who is unseen; and your Father, who sees what is done in secret, will reward you."

WHEN YOU'RE DESPERATE.

TWO

Read 2 Samuel 12. David fasted and prayed for God to save his infant child. This came after being confronted by Nathan about having Uriah killed and taking his wife as his own because she became pregnant with the child that he was asking God to save.

SOME THINGS ONLY CHANGE WHEN WE FAST.

THREE

Read Mark 9:29. This is an encounter of a young boy possessed by demons. Jesus's disciples weren't able to cast them out and this was Jesus's response. "He said unto them, This kind can come forth by nothing, but by prayer and fasting."

WHEN YOU NEED DIVINE PROTECTION.

FOUR

Ezra 8:23 - When Ezra was about to lead a group of exiles back to Jerusalem, he proclaimed a fast in order for the people to seek the Lord earnestly for safe passage. They were to face many dangers without military protection during their nine-hundred-mile journey. "So we fasted and petitioned our God about this, and he answered our prayer."

WHEN YOU NEED GOD'S GUIDANCE.

FIVE

Read Judges 20:26-28; Acts 14:23

WHY SHOULD WE FAST?

WHEN YOU'RE MOURNING.

SIX

Read Nehemiah 1:4-6 Nehemiah mourned the fall of Jerusalem and the children of Israel being taken captive.

TO REPENT AND RETURN TO GOD.

SEVEN

Read Joel 2:12. This is a call to repentance for everyone in light of the coming Day of the Lord. This is speaking of when Jesus returns to take vengeance on those that deny Him as Savior rendering judgment on all of His enemies.

TO HUMBLE YOURSELF BEFORE GOD.

EIGHT

1 Kings 21:27-29 - One of the most wicked men in Jewish history, King Ahab, eventually humbled himself before God and demonstrated it by fasting: "When Ahab heard these words, he tore his clothes, put on sackcloth and fasted. He lay in sackcloth and went around meekly." As a result, God resolved to delay His judgment.

TO OVERCOME TEMPTATIONS.

NINE

Matthew 4:1-11 – Jesus fasted for 40 days and 40 nights and during this time, he privately devoted himself to do the public ministry that was ahead of him.

TO EXPRESS LOVE AND WORSHIP TO GOD.

TEN

Read Luke 2. There's an unforgettable woman whose entire eighty-four years are flashed before us in three verses. Her name is Anna. The summary of her life is found in Luke 2:37: "She never left the temple but worshiped night and day, fasting and praying." As a result, her prayer was answered when she was able to see the Messiah as He was presented after his birth.

99

PRAYER & FASTING

We all deal with difficulties in life and many times what we face seems impossible to overcome. Here are examples of what to pray for as we go deeper in our relationship with the Lord.

Pray for that job you desire.

Pray for your marriage.

Pray for your children.

Pray for your loved ones.

Pray for a deeper relationship with Christ.

Pray for financial freedom.

Pray to forgive the unforgivable.

Pray for release from strongholds.

Pray for complete healing.

IMPORTANCE OF FASTING

Often in the Bible, God's people fasted immediately before a major victory, miracle, or answer to prayer. It prepared them for a blessing

DANIEL FASTED TO RECEIVE GUIDANCE FROM GOD.
Read Daniel 9:3; 21-22; 10:3.

"So I turned to the Lord God and pleaded with him in prayer and petition, in fasting and in sackcloth and ashes." Daniel 9:3 (NIV) "While I was still in prayer, Gabriel, the man I had seen in the earlier vision, came to me in swift flight about the time of the evening sacrifice. He instructed me and said to me, 'Daniel, I have now come to give you insight and understanding.'" Daniel 9:21-22 (NIV)

MOSES FASTED BEFORE RECEIVING THE TEN COMMANDMENTS.
Read Exodus 34:28

"Moses was there with the Lord forty days and forty nights without eating bread or drinking water. And he wrote on the tablets the words of the covenant--the Ten Commandments." Exodus 34:28 (NIV)

QUEEN ESTHER CALLED FOR ALL OF ISRAEL TO FAST.
Read Esther 4:16

"Go, gather together all the Jews who are in Susa, and fast for me. Do not eat or drink for three days, night or day. I and my attendants will fast as you do. When this is done, I will go to the king, even though it is against the law. And if I perish, I perish."

THE ISRAELITES FASTED BEFORE A MIRACULOUS VICTORY.
Read 2 Chronicles 20:2-3

"Some men came and told Jehoshaphat, "A vast army is coming against you from Edom, from the other side of the Sea. It is already in Hazazon Tamar" (that is, En Gedi). Alarmed, Jehoshaphat resolved to inquire of the Lord, and he proclaimed a fast for all Judah." 2 Chronicles 20:2-3 (NIV)

NEHEMIAH FASTED BEFORE BEGINNING THE BUILDING PROJECT
Read Nehemiah 1:4

"When I heard these things, I sat down and wept. For some days I mourned and fasted and prayed before the God of heaven."

NOTES

NOTES

THE
BLOOD
OF
JESUS

THE BLOOD OF JESUS

"And they overcame him by the blood of the Lamb, and by the word of their testimony, and they loved not their lives unto the death." (Revelation 12:11)

"He was despised, and rejected of men; a man of sorrows, and acquainted with grief" Isaiah 53:3. This sounds like someone you know? That's because Jesus took on human flesh. He felt the same emotions you feel, struggled with the same things you struggle with, but without sinning, so that when He shed His Blood for you on the Cross, the power of sin was demolished in the human body.

Jesus, the sacrificial lamb slain for your redemption, will never force Himself on you. He invites you into a relationship with Him. This relationship is not one of judgment but of love. He accepts you fully right where you are today, but He won't leave you in the state that you're in, if you will allow Him to help you do the work of salvation.

Love always leaves a mark. If you accept Jesus's invitation, you will bear His mark. It's that seal placed on you that not only Jesus recognizes but also Satan. He fought Jesus's potential, too. He fought Him all the way to Calvary and beyond. But when Satan encountered Jesus from the grave, he was defeated. So Satan knows the Blood of Jesus from a different perspective than you. He's not the recipient of Grace, you are. He was disarmed through the work of the Cross.

He understands that the Blood of Jesus holds power over him. Jesus pulverized Satan. He didn't just get out of the grave alone. He unlocked the graves of many on that day and they presented themselves to family that knew they were dead, so that there would be witnesses. Will you be a witness and use the blood of Jesus as your weapon against the attacks of Satan?

105

THE BLOOD OF JESUS

1

CLEANSING POWER

The Blood of Jesus possesses cleansing power. If there is any form of dirt or filth in your life or environment, the Blood of Jesus will cleanse them.

2

SANCTIFYING POWER

The Blood of Jesus serves as a disinfectant. It sanitizes your life, your body, house, business, etc.

3

DELIVERANCE POWER

When you apply the Blood of Jesus, it causes the enemy to flee, because the life of God is in it. It sets people free from bondage.

4

HEALING POWER

Jesus took 39 stripes to His body so that it can heal all 39 strands or forms of disease.

5

OVERCOMING POWER

Jesus never told us to fight the devil but to resist him and he will flee from us. This is not defensive but offensive in its approach. You're not afraid of him—you just never engage him.

6

RESURRECTION POWER

It's able to revive anyone or anything that is dead. It could be marriages, finances, businesses, etc.

7

PROTECTION POWER

It's a sword and shield in any circumstance.

THE BLOOD OF JESUS

8 — ACCESS POWER

This gives us the right to and access to open every door that has been closed against the Promises of God.

9 — CREATIVE POWER

This is anything that is supposed to be in the life or body of a person, or has been removed through surgery or witchcraft, and can be recalled back into existence by the Blood of Jesus.

10 — RENEWING POWER

Once we are washed in the Blood of Jesus, we receive His Spirit. It's the Holy Spirit that gives us renewing power. He renews us like the morning.

11 — ANNIHILATION POWER

This type of power is a force that makes the enemy flee in disarray.

12 — BREAKTHROUGH POWER.

Whenever you plead the Blood of Jesus, people and things are set free from any yoke-binding activity.

13 — BURDEN BREAKING POWER

When you plead the Blood of Jesus in any situation, it will bow. We must understand that the weapons for overcoming are found in the word of God. The Bible says: "And they overcame him by the Blood of the Lamb, and by the word of their testimony."

14 — MIRACLE WORKING POWER

Miracles prove that God exists. This type of power manifests in us because of Holy Spirit living in us to perform, healing, casting out of demons, and speaking over weather patterns to cease.

BREAKING DOWN THE

POWER OF THE BLOOD

Every believer has access to the Blood of Jesus as a weapon, but it is through the exercise of it that you gain this level of authority, thereby breaking demonic strongholds.

1

AUTHORITY

We are ambassadors of God with delegated authority. Always maintain your dominion.

HEBREWS 10:19

2

WARFARE

God says our warfare is not of this world; therefore, it cannot be fought with worldly methods. II Corinthians 10:3-6, The weapons of our warfare are not carnal; spiritual warfare is primarily a matter of the mind

EPHESIANS 6:10-18

3

WEAPON

Know your weapons. A weapon is a means of attack or defense. We operate with offensive weapons, which is the Word, the Name, the Blood of Jesus.

EPHESIANS 6:14-17

4

DOMINION

Jesus defeated Satan and gave us dominion. According to Colossians 2:15, Jesus spoiled principalities and powers. Therefore, we are empowered to do the same. I Timothy 6:12 states that we are to fight the good fight of faith

LUKE 10:19

POWER OF THE BLOOD

There are levels to the process of using the Blood of Jesus as a weapon. Don't belittle small beginnings. It's not where you start but where you finish when it comes to spiritual warfare. It's about endurance over perceived skill. This practice is an art, not skill. The might is in the Name of Jesus.

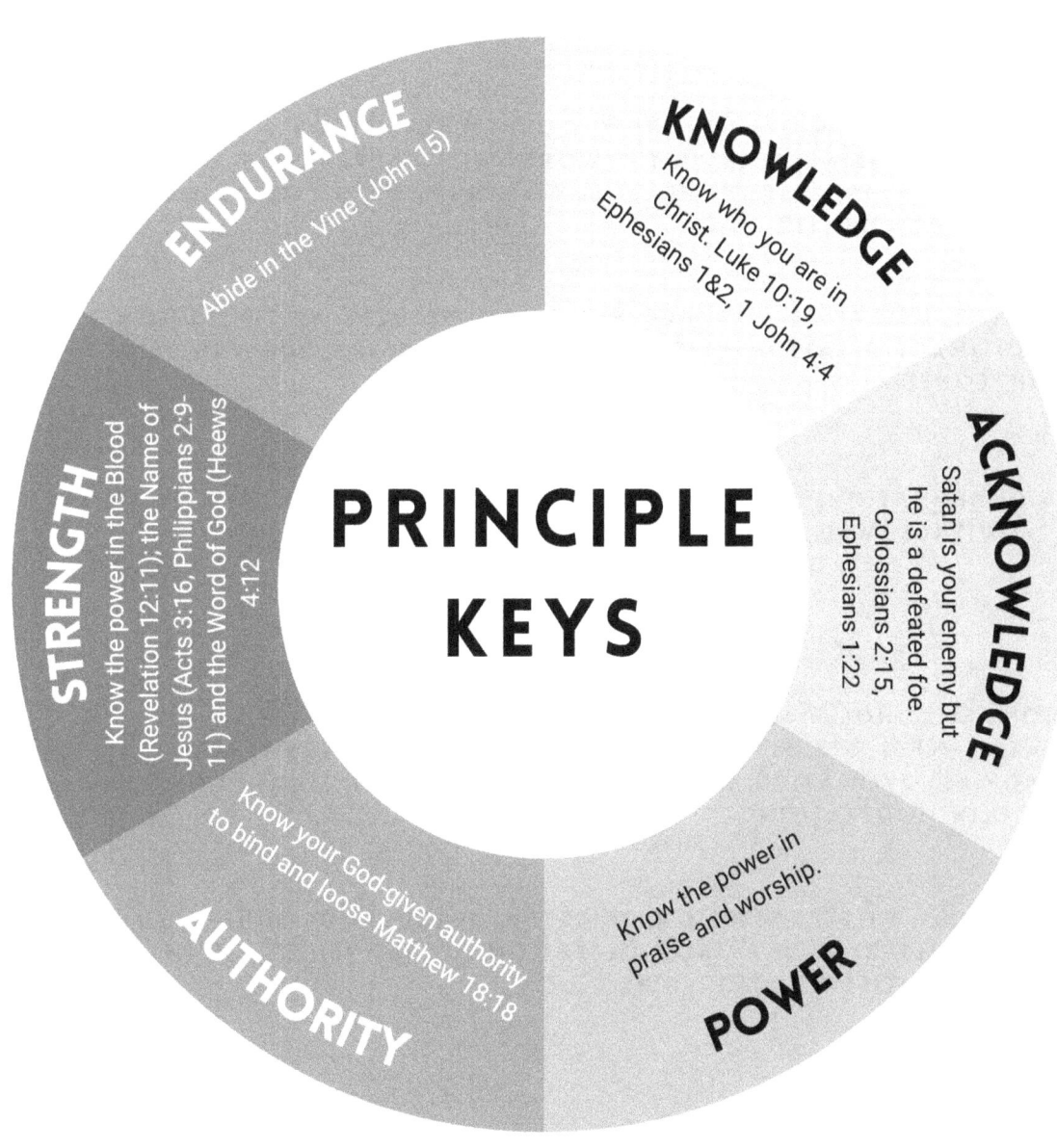

PRINCIPLE KEYS

KNOWLEDGE — Know who you are in Christ. Luke 10:19, Ephesians 1&2, 1 John 4:4

ACKNOWLEDGE — Satan is your enemy but he is a defeated foe. Colossians 2:15, Ephesians 1:22

POWER — Know the power in praise and worship.

AUTHORITY — Know your God-given authority to bind and loose Matthew 18:18

STRENGTH — Know the power in the Blood (Revelation 12:11); the Name of Jesus (Acts 3:16, Philippians 2:9-11) and the Word of God (Heews 4:12

ENDURANCE — Abide in the Vine (John 15)

109

BLOOD OF JESUS

The Blood of Jesus gives us power over circumstances that cause our lives to stall. Here's a list of conditions that we face that the Blood of Jesus gives us authority over. As we go over them, consider how you can use the Blood of Jesus as a weapon against the things that you struggle with.

1 ANGER,HATRED, MALICE, RAGE, MURDER, TEMPER, CURSING, VENGEANCE, RETALIATION, VIOLENCE, ABUSE, CRUELTY, SADISM, UN-FORGIVENESS, BITTERNESS, SELF-RIGHTEOUSNESS, BEING OFFENDED, IRRITABILITY, ANGER TOWARDS OTHERS, ANGER TOWARDS MOTHER OR FATHER, ANGER TOWARDS AUTHORITY, ANGER OR RESENTMENT AGAINST GOD

2 FEAR, FEAR OF MAN, FEAR OF AUTHORITY, DOUBT/UNBELIEF, DREAD, WORRY, ANXIETY, FEAR OF LOSING, FEARING THE WORST WILL HAPPEN, FEAR OF VARIOUS ILLNESSES LIKE CANCER, FEAR PEOPLE WILL GET ANGRY WITH YOU OR WON'T LIKE YOU, FALSE RESPONSIBILITY

3 ABANDONMENT, DESERTION, DIVORCE, REJECTION, NEGLECT, VICTIMIZATION, BLOCKED INTIMACY/RELATIONSHIPS/ENDING RELATIONSHIPS, BURNING BRIDGES, ISOLATION, LONELINESS, SELF-PITY

4 SHAME, CONDEMNATION, DISGRACE, EMBARRASSMENT, GUILT, HATRED, SELF-HATE, SELF-PITY, WITHDRAWAL, HIDING/ANTISOCIAL, TIMIDITY, INFERIORITY

5 ADDICTIONS, ALCOHOL, TOBACCO, DRUGS, FOOD, SUGAR, COFFEE, CHOCOLATE/SWEETS, SEX, FLIRTATION, DIRTY MAGAZINES/WEBSITES/TV SHOWS/MOVIES, OVEREATING, DRINKING TOO MUCH ALCOHOL, ANYTHING YOU CANNOT DO IN MODERATION

6 LYING, CHEATING, THEFT, DECEPTION, TRICKERY, UNTRUSTWORTHINESS, ADULTERY, EMOTIONAL ADULTERY, DENIAL, SELF-DECEPTION, SECRETIVENESS, HIDING PURCHASES/ACTIVITIES/RELATIONSHIPS

7 LACK, FALSE HUMILITY, ROBBING GOD BY NOT TITHING, NOT BELIEVING IN COVENANT BLESSINGS, GREED, COVETOUSNESS, DEBT, DISHONESTY, IDOLATRY OF POSSESSIONS OR PEOPLE, FAILURE

BLOOD OF JESUS

The Blood of Jesus gives us power over circumstances that cause our lives to stall. Here's a list of conditions that we face that the Blood of Jesus gives us authority over. As we go over them, consider how you can use the Blood of Jesus as a weapon against the things that you struggle with.

LUST, FANTASIZING/COVETING ANOTHER'S MATE, FLIRTATION, PREMARITAL SEX, **8**
SEXUAL ABUSE, FORNICATION/ADULTERY/EMOTIONAL ADULTERY, PORNOGRAPHY,
BONDAGE/CONTROL, RAPE, INCEST

DEPRESSION, REJECTION, DESPAIR, HELPLESSNESS, HOPELESSNESS, SADNESS, SELF- **9**
PITY, WITHDRAWAL, SUICIDE

GRIEF, SORROW, DESPAIR, HEARTBREAK, LOSS, PAIN, TORMENT, WEEPING, ANGUISH, **10**
AGONY

PSYCHOLOGICAL DYSFUNCTION, MENTAL ILLNESS, COMPULSIONS, CONFUSION, **11**
HYSTERIA, PARANOIA, SCHIZOPHRENIA, INSANITY, PSYCHOSIS

PRIDE, ARROGANCE, SELFISHNESS, NEED TO CONTROL, PUSHINESS, CALLOUSNESS, **12**
LACK OF CONCERN FOR OTHERS, GOSSIP

PROCRASTINATION, LAZINESS, DISTRACTIONS, CONFUSION, LACK OF FOCUS, **13**
BRASHNESS, NOT THINKING THINGS THROUGH BEFORE ACTING OR SPEAKING,
TARDINESS, DISREGARD FOR OTHERS TIME AND RESOURCES

NOTES

NOTES

FAITH

FAITH AS A WEAPON

Read chapter 6: Between Rocks in "Bulletproof" companion book.

And without faith it is impossible to please him, for whoever would draw near to God must believe that he exists and that he rewards those who seek him. Hebrews 11:6 ESV

When I was a child, I was afraid of everything. I would refuse to go to bed without my sister or my father. It was when I was alone that I would see and hear things that made me frightened. I didn't understand who I was at that time.

Even when I got older, and got married not just the first time but also the second marriage, I was still so afraid. My second husband didn't understand why I needed him to nail all the windows shut. I was so nervous, especially at night because that's when I felt tormented. I thought someone was breaking into our house. I would wake up hearing unexplained noises. I even began seeing shadows of a man turning the corner going from our bedroom to the ensuite.

It wasn't until I received the Holy Spirit that I understood what was happening to me. I was encountering demonic forces and they like to appear at night. The word of God says that Satan is like a roaring lion, roaming around, seeking whom he can swallow up.

The Holy Spirit, living on the inside of me, showed me who I am because I accepted Jesus as my Savior. I gained power from knowing who Satan is and why he's consumed with destroying me, and if he can't destroy me, he wants to at least destroy my potential.

That's why I'm here for you today. I'm here to impress upon you the importance of knowing who Jesus is, why you need Him, then once you accept Him, help you see who you are now.

115

THE FIRST LINE OF DEFENSE

Picture this: The Romans had a skillful trick up their sleeves to block the enemy's fiery arrows, fireballs, and metal projectiles dipped in pitch. They used a shield to protect themselves from the chaos of war and gain the upper hand. But watch out! Sometimes the enemy's tactics can be cleverly disguised as good intentions. This rings true in a classic scripture story where Jesus had to confront Satan himself. "From that time on Jesus began to explain to his disciples that he must go to Jerusalem and suffer many things at the hands of the elders, chief priests, and teachers of the law, and that he must be killed and on the third day be raised to life. Peter took him aside and began to rebuke him. 'Never, Lord!' he said. 'This shall never happen to you!' Jesus turned and said to Peter, 'Get behind me, Satan! You are a stumbling block to me; you do not have in mind the things of God, but the things of men'" (Matt 16:21- 23). Jesus wasn't rebuking Peter, but Satan who was tempting both Him and Peter to disobey God's will. So, let's take a page from Jesus's book and stay alert for disguised tricks from the enemy.

OUR SHIELD GUARDS

Our shield guards us and that shield is faith in God through Jesus the Christ. "Therefore, since we have a great high priest who has gone through the heavens, Jesus the Son of God, let us hold firmly to the faith we profess. For we do not have a high priest who is unable to sympathize with our weaknesses, but we have one who has been tempted in every way, just as we are — yet was without sin. Let us then approach the throne of grace with confidence, so that we may receive mercy and find grace to help us in our time of need" (Hebrews 4:14-16).

116

OUR SHIELD DEFLECTS

With unwavering trust in God and His promises, we can stand like champions, deflecting Satan's fiery arrows that try to mess with our minds and hearts. It's like God has put on a dazzling fireworks show of unbreakable promises to remind us of His love. This unshakable foundation gives us the courage to hold onto hope, even when the seas of life get stormy. As Hebrews 6:17-19 puts it, having faith is like having a sturdy anchor that keeps us grounded, no matter what.

SATAN IS LEFT POWERLESS

The biblical passage in Matthew 4:10-11 recounts an event where Jesus rebuked Satan, stating "Get away from me, Satan! For it is written: 'Worship the Lord your God, and serve him only.'" After this exchange, the devil departed, and angels came to attend to Jesus.

UNITY GIVES US POWER

The Roman army had some genius tricks up their sleeve, especially when it came to shielding themselves from enemy attacks. Whenever the opposing army started shooting arrows at them, the Roman soldiers quickly huddled together in a tight, rectangular formation called the testudo (or the "tortoise"). They'd overlap their shields, creating a wall around the group's perimeter, while the soldiers in the middle would hold their shields above their heads to block any flying arrows. It was like an unstoppable human tank, and only the most monumental efforts could take it down. Even the scripture agrees, "Two can defend themselves, but a cord of three strands is not quickly broken" (Ecclesiastes 4:12).

117

"YOUR ADVERSARY THE DEVIL, AS A ROARING LION, WALKETH ABOUT, SEEKING WHOM HE MAY DEVOUR" 1 PETER 5:8

SATAN KNOWS OUR WEAKNESSES AND HE USES THOSE THINGS TO GET US OFF COURSE FROM GOD'S PLAN

Satan's sneaky tactics involve planting thoughts of surrender in our minds, hoping we'll veer away from obeying God. But guess what? God's love and protection are tied to our obedience to Him. As Genesis 2:16-17 explains, we have free reign to enjoy everything in the garden, but the tree of good and evil is off limits. Deuteronomy 30:15-20 puts it even more simply: We have a choice between life and death, blessings and curses, and the solution is to follow God's commands, love Him, and listen to His voice. Ecclesiastes 12:13 caps it off by stating that our life's duty is to fear God and keep his commandments. And finally, Jesus himself reminds us in John 14:23-24 that if we love Him, we'll obey His teachings. So, let's not give in to Satan's tricks and make living a life of obedience to God our top priority. (Read Genesis 2:16-17; Deuteronomy 30:15-20; Ecclesiastes 12:13; Matthew 28:18-20, and John 14:23-24.)

Satan is like that annoying friend who whispers bad thoughts in your ear. "What if God doesn't exist?" he whispers. "God is not your buddy, and he's surely not good," he hisses. But hey, let's take a step back. Would a good God allow all the chaos and misery we see around us? It's essential to note that God gave us, human beings the right to rule the earth, so it's on us, not Him. (Check out Genesis 1:28-30 for more.) Let's ditch the blame game and work towards living for God, thereby fulfilling His plan.

The devil is always trying to plant negative and spiteful thoughts in our minds, causing a rift between us and our loved ones and even God himself. But, hold up. We have a powerful weapon against this evil scheme, and that's love. As the Bible says, "Love each other as I have loved you" (John 15:12). So, let's spread some love and keep the devil at bay.

TEST OF FAITH

Sometimes God tests our faith by allowing the devil to tempt us. These are examples of when God allowed Satan to tempt good men.

JOB

Job 1:9-12

"Does Job fear [you] for nothing?' Satan replied. 'Have you not put a hedge around him and his household and everything he has? You have blessed the work of his hands so that his flocks and herds are spread throughout the land. But stretch out your hand and strike everything he has, and he will surely curse you to your face.' The Lord said to Satan, 'Very well, then, everything he has is in your hands, but on the man, himself do not lay a finger'"

FIRST

PETER

Luke 22:31-32

Peter was allowed to be sifted like wheat, "Simon, Simon, Satan has asked to sift you as wheat. But I have prayed for you, Simon, that your faith may not fail. And when you have turned back, strengthen your brothers"

SECOND

JESUS

Luke 4:1-2

"Jesus, full of the Holy Spirit, returned from the Jordan and was led by the Spirit in the wilderness for forty days, being tempted by the devil. And he ate nothing during those days. And when they ended, he was hungry."

THIRD

YOUR CHALLENGE

Satan works to get us to have thoughts of lust, wrath, revenge, or despair, which can cripple our ability to resist Satan's strategies. According to Proverbs 6:16-19, a list is compiled below of behaviors that reflect that Satan is at work in us or others. In the space provided write down how you have been effected by these habits.

ONE

A PROUD LOOK

TWO

A LYING TONGUE

THREE

HANDS THAT SHED INNOCENT BLOOD

FOUR

A HEART THAT DEVISES WICKED PLOTS

FIVE

FEET THAT HUSTLE TO GET INTO TROUBLE

SIX

A LYING WITNESS WHO SPEAKS FALSEHOODS

SEVEN

SOMEONE WHO STIRS UP CONFLICT AMONG FAMILY OR FRIENDS

120

YOUR TEST OF FAITH

Satan wants us to have sudden fears, anxieties, panic attacks, and feeling like nothing is right, especially with God. How have these feelings overwhelmed you?

QUESTIONS:	WRITE YOUR ANSWERS HERE...
Have you experienced anxiety, panic attacks, alarming fear that is unexplainable? What caused it?	
Have your or a family member been stricken with medical attacks, like the case with Job? What happened?	
Have you had doubts that God would want to save or use you?	
Have you had doubts about Jesus Christ standing in the gap for you?	
Do you question whether or not God and Jesus Christ are real?	
Do you believe that God has given us authority as discussed in this material?	
Did something happen in your life that caused you to be suspicious of these facts?	
Do you believe that Jesus is still alive today and living in Heaven? Do you believe that there is a heaven?	

NOTES

NOTES

LOVE AND UNITY

LOVE AND UNITY

Read chapter 9: Drive in "Bulletproof" companion book.

Merriam-Webster.com defines love as a strong affection for another arising out of kinship or personal ties; warm attachment, enthusiasm, or devotion; affection based on admiration, benevolence, or common interests; the object of attachment, devotion, or admiration.

The Bible gives a definition of love in the New Testament. 1 Corinthians 13:4-7 NKJV states, "Love suffers long and is kind; love does not envy; love does not parade itself, is not puffed up; does not behave rudely, does not seek its own, is not provoked, thinks no evil; does not rejoice in iniquity, but rejoices in the truth; bears all things, believes all things, hopes all things, endures all things." Love never fails.

How can love and unity be a weapon used to disarm our enemies? These two elements are strong forces against Satan because Jesus said in Matthew 18:19 that if two believers residing on earth agree on anything that they pray to God for, it will be done for them. He said that whatever we bind on earth is already bound in heaven and whatever we loose on earth, is already loosed in heaven. That means there is greater authority and evidence of answered prayers when we are unified in our love for God and each other. When that relationship causes two people to join forces by praying to God to bind something, at the moment it is spoken, it is already done for them from the portals of heaven.

That means we must let go of the offenses done that hurt us. Satan stirred up division among us, causing us to be at odds with each other to divide us. All he wants is to render us powerless because he knows our strength when we are on one accord. There's power in our agreement.

"A new command I give you: Love one another. As I have loved you, so you must love one another. By this everyone will know that you are my disciples, if you love one another."
John 13:34-35

"THE TWO
MOST
POWERFUL
WARRIORS
ARE
PATIENCE
AND TIME."

- LEO TOLSTOY

TYPES OF LOVE

There are 8 different types or characteristics of love. Below, each type is listed along with a brief description of what it characterizes.

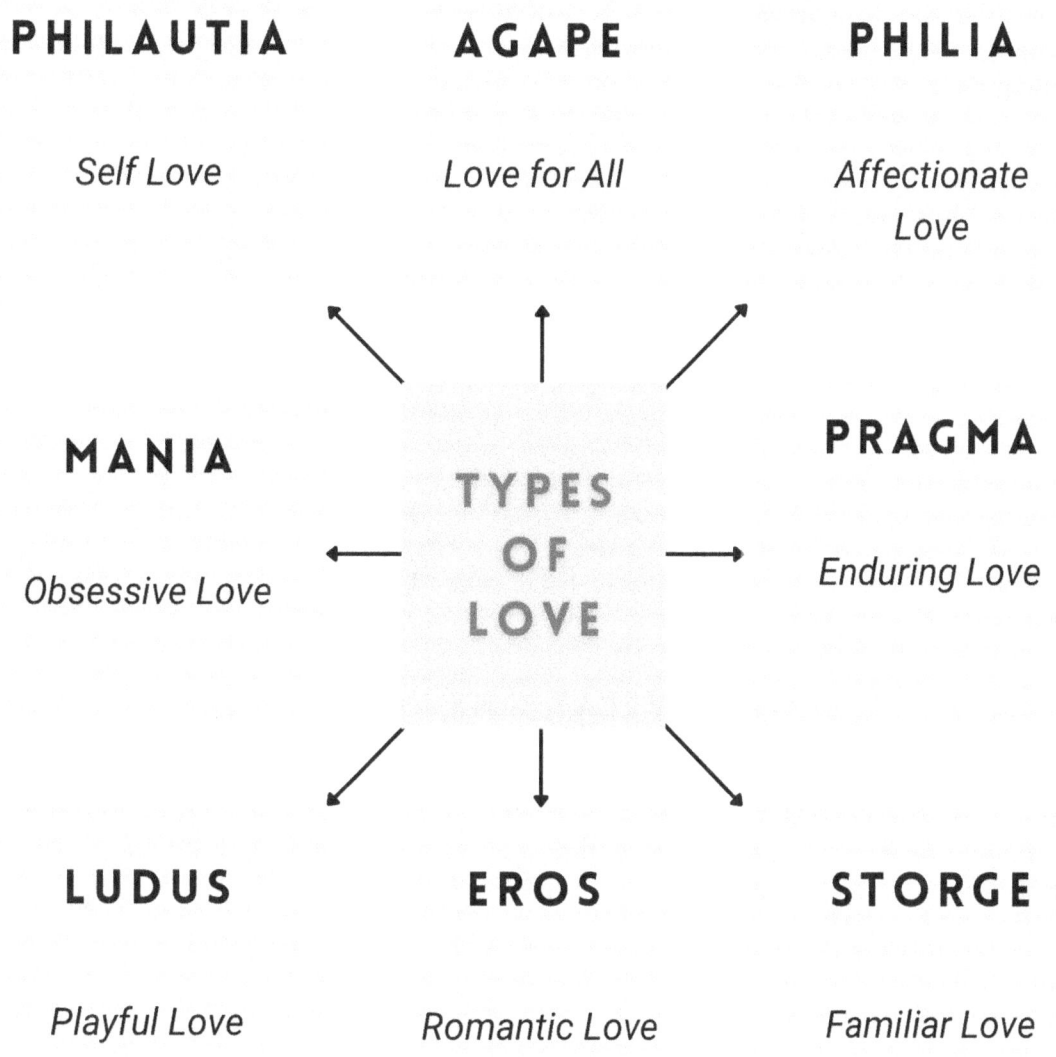

PHILAUTIA

Self Love

AGAPE

Love for All

PHILIA

Affectionate Love

MANIA

Obsessive Love

TYPES OF LOVE

PRAGMA

Enduring Love

LUDUS

Playful Love

EROS

Romantic Love

STORGE

Familiar Love

When we discuss Love and Unity as a weapon, we are referring to Agape or Philia Love. Agape love involves making a decision to love. Philia involves friendship or fondness but does not include intimate love.

NEGATIVE SIDE TO LOVE

Love is a beautiful thing but there can be negative aspects to love when speaking of agape type love. Read the scripture references then answer the corresponding questions.

READ LUKE 6:32-33 - SINNERS LOVE THOSE WHO LOVE THEM.

How does the biblical concept, 'Sinners love those who love them,' illuminate the spiritual and moral aspects of relationships, shedding light on the nature of love and forgiveness within the context of this scripture?

READ MATTHEW 24:12; REVELATIONS 2:4

How does this warning that 'Love can grow cold.' (Matthew 24:12) and the call to return to our 'first love,' which is Christ, as emphasized in Revelation 2:4, provide insights into the spiritual journey, challenges to faith, and the importance of maintaining a fervent love for Christ in the face of potential deterioration?

LOVE CAN BE EVIL

Let's take a look at how love can be evil. Read the scripture references then answer the corresponding questions.

READ JOHN 3:19 THEN ANSWER THE FOLLOWING QUESTION.

How does the statement that 'Men love darkness' resonate with what you know about human nature, sin, and the transformative power of embracing the light of faith and righteousness found in Jesus?

1

READ JOHN 12:43 THEN ANSWER THE FOLLOWING QUESTION.

How does understanding the inclination of men to seek praise align with using love as a weapon, and what insights does it offer into the challenges of humility and the pursuit of righteousness because of your faith in Jesus?

2

READ 2 TIMOTHY 3:2 THEN ANSWER THE FOLLOWING QUESTION.

How does the statement that 'men love themselves' relate to the emphasis on selflessness, humility, and the challenge of loving others as oneself in your spiritual journey?

3

READ 2 TIMOTHY 3:2 THEN ANSWER THE FOLLOWING QUESTION.

How does this statement that 'people will be lovers of themselves' demonstrate the dangers of materialism and the pursuit of wealth? How does this insight challenge you in relationship to the concept of love and unity as a weapon?

4

WE ARE OBLIGATED TO LOVE

"You shall love the Lord your God with all your heart and with all your soul and with all your might." Deuteronomy 6:5 ESV

In Mark 12:29-34, Jesus emphasizes the greatest commandment, which is to love God above all and love your neighbor as yourself. This underlines the significance of acknowledging God's power, kindness, and the unique relationship between the Creator and His creation. The Scriptures remind us that love is a divine gift from God, which inspires us to reciprocate by loving Him back. Our love for God becomes both a spiritual obligation and a way of expressing our gratitude for the boundless love bestowed upon us. This mutual love forms the foundation of a meaningful relationship between us and God, highlighting the inseparable connection between love, faith, and devotion within the community of faith.

We are to love God with our whole heart, mind, soul, and strength. How can we do that when we've never seen God and He lives in heaven? By loving others. By showing kindness to those in need. By helping the widows and the motherless or fatherless. By taking care of the sick and those in prison. Jesus said whenever you have done good deeds for the least of these, you have done it for me. (Matthew 25:40-45 NIV) This is a supernatural love. You love what you've never seen before.

It's out of this love for God and our fellow man that causes us to pray fervently for those that need answers that only God can give. Our prayers are an expression of our love for each other.

130

LOVING GOD BRINGS REWARD

According to John 8:42, when we love Christ, we show love for the Father. With this love, comes much in the form of rewards. The following is an abbreviated list of the rewards for loving God.

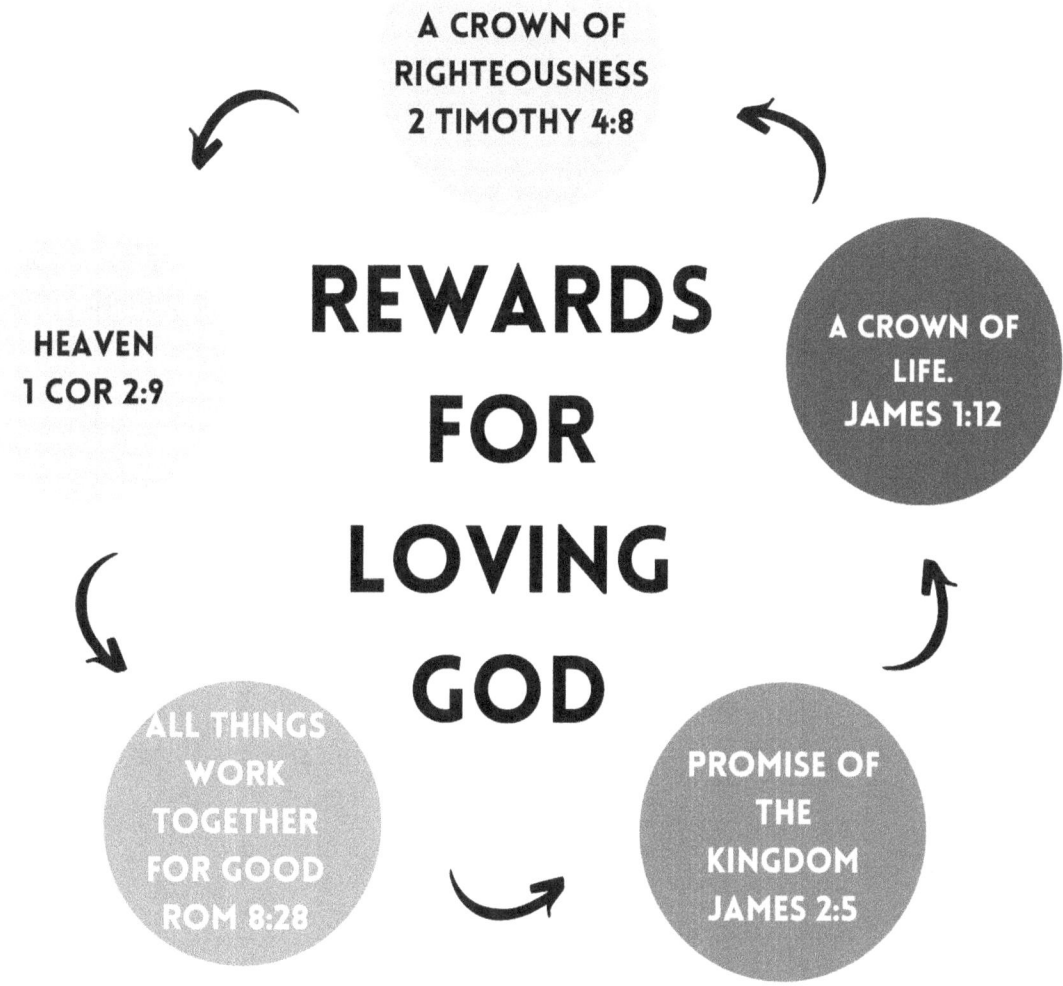

A CROWN OF RIGHTEOUSNESS
2 TIMOTHY 4:8

HEAVEN
1 COR 2:9

REWARDS FOR LOVING GOD

A CROWN OF LIFE.
JAMES 1:12

ALL THINGS WORK TOGETHER FOR GOOD
ROM 8:28

PROMISE OF THE KINGDOM
JAMES 2:5

This love is discreet, which causes kingdom derived dominion and is produced out of a personal relationship with Christ. It goes beyond just church attendance. It's about spending time with the Lord, being silent in His presence, and waiting for His responses. He wants a relationship with you more than you want it with Him. Make time on your calendar daily to meditate on one scripture, pray then be silent to hear.

131

LOVE ONE ANOTHER

We are obligated to love one another. What should that look like? Read the following scriptures and answer the corresponding questions.

READ JOHN 13:34

How does the concept of "loving one another" as a new commandment, as emphasized in the Scriptures, challenge and redefine traditional notions of morality, compassion, and interpersonal relationships within the context of love and unity as a weapon?

READ JOHN 13:35

How does Jesus's declaration, "By this all will know that you are My disciples, if you have love for one another," illuminate the significance of love as a defining characteristic of discipleship, and what implications does this statement hold for the identity and mission of the Christian community in the world?

READ 1 JOHN 2:11

How can we achieve love and unity when it is undermined by spiritual darkness and interpersonal hatred? What are the consequences for harboring animosity? What insights does it provide into the transformative nature of love and forgiveness as a weapon against the wiles of Satan?

READ JOHN 15:12 & 15:17

What role does the commandment to "love one another" play in fostering unity and understanding among individuals of different faiths? Is it possible to promote peace and cooperation even in the face of differing beliefs within the same faith? Why did Jesus place so much emphasis on loving one another?

LOVE ONE ANOTHER

We are obligated to love one another. What should that look like? Read the following scriptures and answer the corresponding questions.

READ 2 CORINTHIANS 2:4,8

Why does Paul, in this scripture, urge the Corinthian church to reaffirm their love for a fallen brother among them?

READ 1 JOHN 4:11

How does God's example of love set forth a moral imperative for all believers, and what role does this command play in shaping the character and actions of individuals within Christian communities?

READ ROMANS 13:8

How does the command to love function as a foundational framework for all believers in Jesus, and what are the implications of this teaching for interpersonal relationships and ethical conduct in the lives of believers?

GOING DEEPER

It's easy to love those who love us. It's a challenge to show love to those who we don't know. It's even more difficult to love those who hate and do harmful things to us. Go deeper by reading these scriptures and answering the questions associated with them. Be transparent about your feelings.

READ MATTHEW 19:19 AND JAMES 2:8

Based on these scriptures, who is our neighbor? How does it say we are to love them? How is this possible? From James 2:8, what is the royal law that is referenced?

READ MATTHEW 5:44

How does this scripture, which instructs us to 'love your enemies and pray for those who persecute you,' challenge us to embrace a mindset of compassion and forgiveness towards those who may oppose or harm us?

Knowing God Through Love

Beloved, let us love one another, for love is of God; and everyone who loves is born of God and knows God. He who does not love does

When trying to understand how we can love our enemies, it's good to delve into God's love for us. He sacrificed His Son while we were His enemies. Let that sink in.

The pages of the Bible are bursting with God's ultimate love story, a tale that captures His heart and His relationship with us. It's like a beautiful tapestry, with each thread weaving a different dimension of God's love. The Father's love is front and center, shining bright in John 3:16, where He gives up His son for us. And don't forget Ephesians 2:4, where God's love is so rich in mercy, it's like a never-ending waterfall of compassion.

But wait, there's more! The Son's love is just as powerful, seen in Mark 10:21, where He shows us love through His actions and teachings. This love reaches its pinnacle with His ultimate sacrifice on the cross, which shows us the true meaning of selfless love. It's also like a marriage, where both partners give their all, like in Ephesians 5:25. This is the kind of love showcased in 1 John 3:16.

The best part? This love comes from the Holy Spirit, and it's not something we can ever earn. It's a gift, and we just have to accept it with open arms. So let's bask in the glow of God's love, it's the ultimate heartwarming experience!

God's love is extensive, but it is not without discipline. Hebrews 12:6 highlights that God's love comes with chastening, which is an indication of His commitment to our spiritual development and transformation.

Romans 8:38-39 affirms that nothing can break the bond between us and God's love. This love is all-embracing, protecting us from any force that may attempt to sever our connection with the Divine. This truth anchors us, providing comfort and security in the face of life's uncertainties.

The New Testament underscores the unbreakable link between love and obedience. John 14:31 succinctly communicates that Jesus loves the Father and obeys His commands. Obedience becomes the tangible expression of love, reinforcing the idea that true love naturally leads to a desire to fulfill the will of the One we love. This emphasis on obedience as proof of love echoes throughout the New Testament, emphasizing the transformative power of God's love in shaping our actions and attitudes.

LOVE IS ATTAINABLE

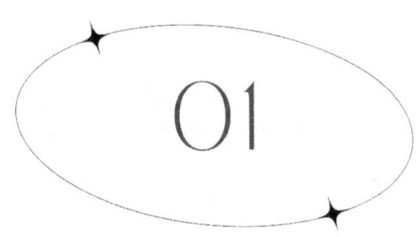

STEP ONE

THOSE WHO ARE FORGIVEN MUCH MUST ALSO LOVE MUCH. LUKE 7:42-43.

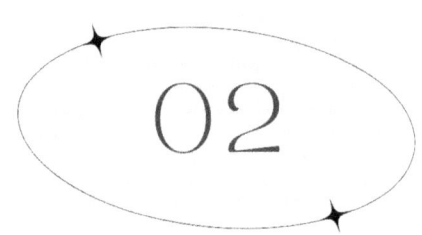

STEP TWO

THIS TYPE OF LOVE HAS BEEN POURED INTO OUR HEARTS. ROMANS 5:5.

STEP THREE

LOVE IS PART OF THE FRUIT OF THE SPIRIT. GALATIANS 5:22; ROMANS 15:30.

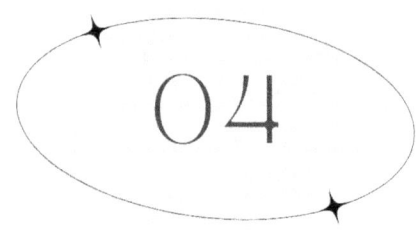

STEP FOUR

WE ARE TO GIVE CHARITY. COLOSSIANS 3: 14.

STEP FIVE

WE MUST DEMONSTRATE AGAPE LOVE. JOHN 15:9.

LOVE'S MANY LAYERS

*Love is a verb, not a noun. It's not just a person, place or thing. It is demonstrated through action as seen through our relationship with God. For God loved us so much, that He **gave** His son...*

- [ ] God is love. I John 4:8, 16.

- [ ] Love is a decision. Deuteronomy 30:20

- [ ] Love is faithful. 1 Corinthians 13

- [ ] Love is shared. Philippians 2:2

- [ ] Love is like yeast.

- [ ] Love is learned. I Thessalonians 4:9, I Timothy 4: 12

- [ ] Love is pursued. I Timothy 6: 11

- [ ] Love is stimulated. Hebrews 10:24

- [ ] Love grows and multiplies. Jude 2; Ephesians 3:17

- [ ] Love is longsuffering. I Corinthians 13:4

- [ ] Love can be received. I John 4: 16

- [ ] Love is kind. I Corinthians 13:4

- [ ] Love is not possessive. I Corinthians 13:4

LOVE'S MANY LAYERS

*Love is a verb, not a noun. It's not just a person, place or thing. It is demonstrated through action as seen through our relationship with God. For God loved us so much, that He **gave** His son...*

- [ ] Love is humble. I Corinthians 13:4

- [ ] Love is not provoked. I Corinthians 13:5

- [ ] Love bears all things. I Corinthians 13:7, Ephesians 4:2

- [ ] Love believes all things. I Corinthians 13:7

- [ ] Love hopes. I Corinthians 13:7

- [ ] Love produces good behavior. I Corinthians 13:6

- [ ] Love is faithful. I Corinthians 13:8

- [ ] Love is perfect. I Corinthians 13:10, Ephesians 4: 11

- [ ] Love abounds. Philippians 1:9

- [ ] Love comforts. Philippians 2:1, Colossians 2:2

- [ ] Love is active. I Thessalonians 1:3

- [ ] Love protects. I Thessalonians 5:8

- [ ] Love is not diluted. John 15:13-17

LOVE'S MANY LAYERS

*Love is a verb, not a noun. It's not just a person, place or thing. It is demonstrated through action as seen through our relationship with God. For God loved us so much, that He **gave** His son...*

- [ ] Love is compassionate. I John 3: 17

- [ ] Love drives out fear. I John 4: 18

- [ ] Love sacrifices. I Corinthians 13:3

- [ ] Love thinks no evil—it takes the high road. I Corinthians 13:5

- [ ] Love does not rejoice in wrong. I Corinthians 13:6

- [ ] Love has the capacity to exceed faith and hope. I Corinthians 13:13

- [ ] Love holds universal application in life. I Corinthians 16:14

- [ ] Love is limitless and all encompassing. I Corinthians 16:14

- [ ] Love covers a multitude of sin. I Peter 4:8

- [ ] Love won't grow cold.

- [ ] Love won't quit. Galatians 5:6

- [ ] Love is supreme. I Peter 4:8

NOTES

NOTES

FORGIVENESS AND REPENTANCE

FORGIVENESS AND REPENTANCE

LET IT GO

"I'm right." "No. You're wrong. I'm right." Have you ever been in this type of discourse with someone that you really care about? You go round and round rehashing the details of what you both thought happened. At the end, the conversation becomes a heated argument and then you're both angry with each other. How does it end? Does one of you give in and apologize, although you are certain that you're right? Upon further evaluation, do you consider that the argument isn't worth jeopardizing the relationship? Or do you hold grudges and not let go of it? Weighed in the balance, the relationship should be far more important than whatever the disagreement was about.

At this point, it becomes about repentance--saying I'm sorry or I apologize then making a decision about how you will relate with each other in the future. That's all that repentance is. It's confessing what you've done wrong and turning away from doing it in the future.

Forgiveness is the tough part. It's the letting go part that we struggle with. But letting go is exactly what we need to do because unity is more important than our feelings about what happened.

Read chapter 4: Inside Job in "Bulletproof" companion book.

"But I say to you that whoever is angry with his brother without a cause shall be in danger of the judgment."
Matthew 5:22

LEVIATHAN

*"Can you pull in Leviathan with a fishhook
or tie down its tongue with a rope?...It looks down on all that are haughty; it is
king over all that are proud." Job 41:1;34*

When I was in high school, I was absorbed in all things related to music. I sang in the choir and ensemble and I was pretty good at it. I had been taking voice lessons since I was in the seventh grade and had already performed on several stages because of my voice teacher giving me opportunities to showcase my talent.

But I became consumed with my own abilities. Deep down inside, I knew I was the best and those feelings began to show up when I had to relate to others. But as a Christian, I felt the need to have humility, although it was really fake.

I remember the first time I lost a singing contest. It was at a single's conference in Los Angeles. I ended up losing the contest to someone that I thought was inferior to me. I made snide remarks about the fact that I was the best thing they had on stage but a friend reminded me that pride goes before a fall and I was full of it.

I still didn't do anything about this silent killer living on the inside of me. Pride was eating away at my potential best and I was feeding it daily. I couldn't see how it was effecting me and everyone around me.

144

"UNTAMED PRIDE BECOMES A RUNAWAY TRAIN."

- LAURAINE WHITE

That's what pride will do, if you let it. It becomes a runaway train. And you know what happens with them--they end up derailed.

My issue? I never considered that I was dealing with "the pride of life." I was taught at an early age that this was wrong and I really didn't consider that I had a problem. Until 2014, when my mother passed away and my husband and I separated.

I was alone. It was in that place of solitude that the Holy Spirit became my best friend and confidante. As a friend, Holy Spirit led me to understand that I was full of pride and He led me on a journey of discovery that I will never forget.

He showed me how I had a need to always be right. I was never wrong. I always had to have the last word in an argument. I was always correcting other people because I knew everything and I liked to receive honor from others for my singing abilities. I just couldn't celebrate the abilities in others. I was self centered and liked drawing attention to myself, no matter how much "false" humility I tried to exhibit in public. I was full of it.

I had to become transparent with myself. At the end of this encounter with the Holy Spirit, I was in tears. I saw myself for the first time for who I really was. I was not all that I proclaimed to be. I was allowing pride to take over my life.

That was the first time that I ever heard the word, Leviathan. I had to google the name and when I did, I found little information on it. I did find several scriptures that mentioned it but I needed the Holy Spirit to guide my study of the subject.

The first reference that I found was in Job 41. The preceding chapters involved God reprimanding Job, who was considered a good, devout Jew. But God said that Job was dealing with Leviathan, the king of all who are **proud**. In essence, God confronted the pride in Job so that he would repent of it.

I was stumped because that included me! I, too, was dealing with pride. I had to dig for more about who this Leviathan was so that I could be free of him.

He is that "twisted serpent" mentioned in Isaiah 27:1 NASB that God will destroy at the end of Time that is also referenced in Revelation. In Revelation, the reference is to a beast but it is one in the same spirit. It's one of pride. It's a being that elevates itself above God on earth and at that time everyone will worship this being that is full of pride.

Upon reading this, I knew I wanted no part of this spirit. I needed to be free. But how? I had no one to show me so the Holy Spirit led me to a process of freedom from Leviathan's choke-hold on me.

It wasn't long after having this encounter with the Holy Spirit that I had a dream about encountering Satan in a church. As soon as I entered, there were people running around, like chickens with their heads chopped off. I engaged in conversation with Satan in this dream instead of recognizing who he was. All I saw was a handsome man who was the only one that stopped to speak with me. You know we always get tripped up by a handsome face.

Ignorance is not bliss. At the end of the dream, I began to realize who I was dealing with. His appearance began to change and he became grotesque. At that point, I realized who he was and was cautious about how I moved next.

Realizing that I was on to him, Satan asked me to pick up the gun that was on the floor. As I went to pick it up, he pulled out a machete then I woke up. As I awakened, I heard the Spirit say, "you don't entertain demons. You cast them out."

What the Holy Spirit showed me was that casting out Leviathan is an internal work. You cast him out of *you* by your repentance from specific things. And that repentance leads to freedom from Leviathan.

The keys to freedom involve knowing who he is, identifying his characteristics, in you and in others, then the Holy Spirit will lead you to the path of cleansing.

146

FINDING FREEDOM FROM LEVIATHAN

The spirit of Leviathan twists communication between people that causes division. It can break up marriages, families, businesses, and churches. When caught up in it, it seems that everything in your communication gets twisted, going back and forth causing sheer chaos.

When prolonged possession of these twisted encounters occur, it can even cause you to be inflicted with disease. This comes because it causes you to harbor unforgiveness in your heart.

But remember, one of the spiritual weapons we have as believers in Jesus, is our love and unity. We become ineffective when there is discord and chaos between us; thereby, diluting the power of God at work in us.

The following pages will give an outline of how the Holy Spirit led me to be free of Leviathan. The freedom that I experienced even caused my countenance to change and everyone around me noticed how I was transformed. Remember, it wasn't until after Job repented of having pride and prayed for his friends that God restored him.

147

"YOU MUST NOT FIGHT TOO OFTEN WITH ONE ENEMY, OR YOU WILL TEACH HIM ALL OF YOUR ART OF WAR."

- NAPOLEON BONAPARTE

148

FORGIVENSS

Forgiveness is a choice and that makes it a weapon. When you choose to forgive, you take the power away from Satan and you become empowered through the Blood of Jesus to conquer sin in your own life. When you forgive, God forgives you.

STEP ONE

BE DELIBERATE

This choice must be deliberate because of the ensuing emotions that follow the decision.

Colossians 3:13, Luke 6:37

STEP TWO

THEY'RE NOT OFF THE HOOK

It doesn't mean that what they did is okay but you choose to keep your soul free from offenses.

Matthew 18:21-22, Psalm 103:10

STEP THREE

IT CANCELS DEBT

The choice to forgive cancels out the "spiritual" debt that is owed by the person that caused the offense.

Mark 11:25, Ephesians 2:4-5

149

SIGNS OF PRIDE

Choosing not to forgive opens the door to Satan's attacks and keeping us from the freedom in Christ that we desire and deserve. This choice creates the environment that cause us to have things in common with the spirit of Leviathan. (References: Job 3:8, Job 41:1-34, Psalm 74:14, Isaiah 27:1) They are:

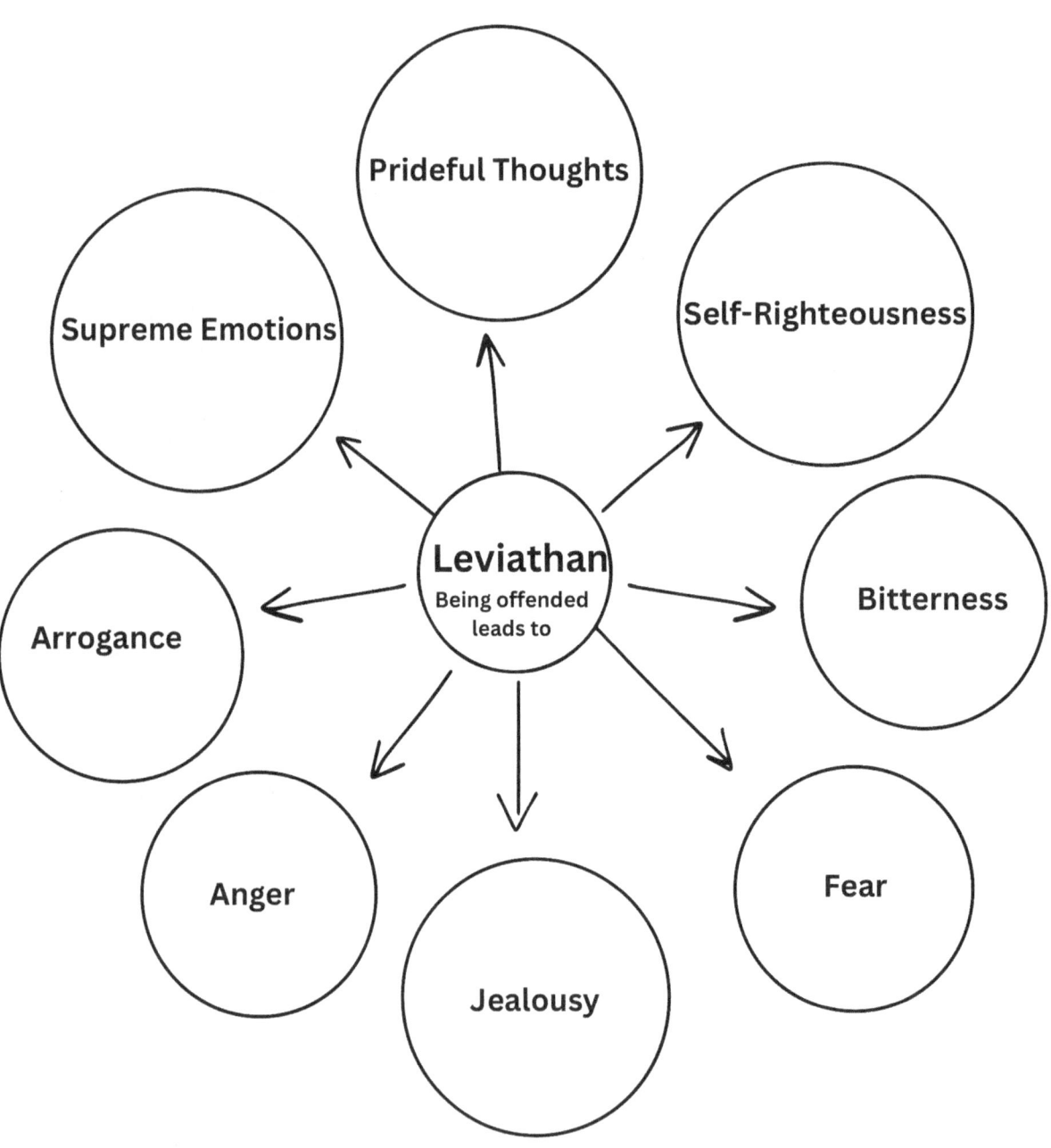

SIGNS OF PRIDE

1 — "I'M TOO GOOD FOR THIS."

Whether it's because of your title or position, you feel that doing what is asked of you is beneath you. It may be on the job or at home, but performing menial tasks is something we all must do.

2 — YOU ARE TOO PROUD TO ASK FOR HELP.

Your independence is one thing, but when it becomes a matter of not admitting that you are dealing with something that is beyond your ability to handle, it becomes prideful.

3 — YOU THINK TOO HIGHLY OF YOURSELF.

You are absorbed with your accomplishments and no one can get a word in edge-wise. That's pride. Sometimes it's more subtle. In your mind you secretly think you're better than others because of your background or experiences.

4 — YOU'RE ALWAYS PUTTING OTHER PEOPLE DOWN.

Being overly critical is a sign that deep down inside, you need to feel better about yourself. Most times, you can't see that you do the same things but you feel that you're better. So...

5 — YOU'RE UNABLE TO ACCEPT CONSTRUCTIVE CRITICISM.

When being criticized, your first thought is, "They're just jealous," you're dealing with pride. Your struggle to receive someone else's critical assessment of what you can do better is a sign of pride.

6 — YOU HAVE DIFFICULTY IN SUBMITTING TO AUTHORITY.

Whether it is at home, on the job, or at church, you struggle with accepting the person that has authority over you. You feel you can do a better job than them. This is a sign of pride.

7 — YOU TALK ABOUT YOURSELF A LOT.

Social media causes us all to struggle with this. But if you feel that you can only post extremely great information about yourself and nothing else, it's a sign of pride. Take a long hard look at your behaviors in this area.

151

BREAKING DOWN THE
STEPS TO FREEDOM

STEP ONE

I repent for being prideful and bitter; I ask you Lord Jesus to cleanse my thoughts and emotions of all bitterness, anger, and pride. Set my emotions free, in Jesus Name. Amen.

STEP TWO

I repent of saying bitter and prideful things to other people. Forgive me for always thinking I'm right and everyone else is wrong. Cleanse my thoughts so that I turn away from such behavior, in Jesus name I ask this. Amen.

STEP THREE

I humble myself before you, Jesus, and I ask that you heal my soul of these sins. Heal and cleanse me from the sins of pride that give Leviathan access to my soul.

STEP FOUR

I forgive the person(s) that I'm in conflict with and I confess that they do not owe me anything. I free them from any emotional or spiritual debt they owe me.

STEP FIVE

I repent for the part that I have played in the chaos and confusion caused through Leviathan's twisting of our communication. I decree that I am free from all attachment to Leviathan and pride, in Jesus's name. Amen.

FREEDOM

THE UNFORGIVING SERVANT

Read Matthew 18:21-35. It's the story of the unforgiving servant and how the King forgave him. But given the opportunity to forgive the debts of someone that owes him, he has no mercy. Let's see what the outcome is. Then we will assess how this correlates to us.

THE KING AND THE SERVANT (MATTHEW 18:21-35)

The Situation ☐ The king was owed an amount so large the servant could never repay.

The Servants' Plea ☐ The servant admitted his debt and begged for mercy.

The Response ☐ The king felt compassion for the servant and released the debt.

THE UNFORGIVING SERVANT AND ANOTHER SERVANT

The Situation ☐ He was owed a small amount by one of his peers. He grabbed the one that owed a small amount and choked him, having no compassion.

The Servants' Plea ☐ The indebted servant begged for mercy.

The Response ☐ He refused, demanded payment, and put him in a place where he would never be able to repay.

THE KING AND THE UNFORGIVING SERVANT

The Situation ☐ The king heard of the ungrateful servants refusal to forgive another servant what was owed him.

The King's Response ☐ The King had him thrown into prison and tortured until he could repay.

The Response ☐ Jesus warns that this is how God will treat us when we don't forgive.

THE KING AND US

The Situation ☐ We choose to hold onto grudges against those who have done us wrong.

The King's Plea ☐ Forgive, as I have forgiven you. If you don't forgive, I won't forgive you.

Our Response ☐ ???

153

FORGIVENESS

We can never repay God what we owe. When someone else does evil to us, they can never repay either. But when we offer our forgiveness, we don't hold them accountable for their evil. When we refuse to forgive someone else, it's the same as saying, "I would never do such a thing." When we realize our own evil, we know that we can and will do the same things to others.

What about the person that doesn't seek forgiveness and won't repent? Remember, Jesus forgave us while we were His enemies. He died on the Cross in spite of those standing, watching, and mocking Him. They did not know what they were doing. Until they repented, there would be no remission of their sin and no relationship with the Father. But what forgiveness does is releases the other person from owing us a spiritual debt. It turns the problem over to God. We no longer hold it in our power to judge.

154

FORGIVENESS & REPENTANCE

Read Job 3:8; 40:15; 41:26, Amos 9:3, Psalm 74:13-23; 104:26, Isaiah 27:1, Matthew 6:14-15; 9:13; 18:21-35, 2 Corinthians 10:4-6, Mark 1:14, Acts 2:37; 17:30, Luke 15:7-10. Now answer the following questions.

How do the references to Leviathan contribute to the broader understanding of forgiveness and repentance, and what significance do these passages hold in relation to God's mercy and justice?

1

How does forgiveness as articulated by Jesus establish a reciprocal relationship between our forgiveness and God's forgiveness, and what implications does this have regarding the challenges of forgiving others in our lives?

2

How does the parable of the unforgiving servant shed light on God's expectation for believers to extend forgiveness to others, and what consequences are outlined for those who choose not to embrace forgiveness in their interactions with others? (Matthew 18:21-35)

3

How do the New Testament passages emphasize repentance, and how does repentance serve as a transformative and redemptive process in the lives of individuals seeking reconciliation with God?

4

How does the call to repentance intersect with the broader narrative of forgiveness, and what role does genuine repentance play in fostering a renewed relationship with God?

5

155

SPIRITUAL WEAPONS

KEY TAKEAWAYS

- Truth

- Praise and worship

- Prayer

- The Blood of Jesus

- Faith

- Love and Unity

- Forgiveness and Repentance

These are the seven spiritual weapons discussed in this section of the Master class. It is important to recognize each of them individually so that you are fully armed to fight the spiritual battles that you must face.

In all of your getting, get an understanding of what these elements mean for you. Before delving into any of these things, we discussed the importance of having a relationship with Jesus and the Holy Spirit. These spiritual weapons mean absolutely nothing without them leading you to know what's up ahead for you and how you are to respond.

Just as a carpenter, building a house will not use every tool in his tool box in every situation he has to face in order to complete his assignment, we, too, will not necessarily use every tool, every time we face our enemy. The Holy Spirit will lead you as you progress in the things of the spirit. Do not doubt that He's for you. Trust Him.

156

NOTES

NOTES

NOTES

SECTION 5: SIGNS OF A BELIVER

SIGNS
OF A
BELIEVER

"These signs will accompany those who have believed: in My name, they will cast out demons, they will speak with new tongues; they will pick up serpents, and if they drink any deadly poison, it will not harm them; they will lay hands on the sick, and they will recover."

Mark 16:15-18

SIGNS OF A BELIEVER

Read chapter 11: Keep Going in "Bulletproof" companion book.

Then Jesus asked, "What is the kingdom of God like? What shall I compare it to? It is like a mustard seed, which a man took and planted in his garden. It grew and became a tree, and the birds perched in its branches." Luke 13:18-19

Would you assume that a tree is alive because it has leaves on it? Don't let the green foliage on the tree trip you up. There will be signs that show whether the tree is alive or dead, even when it has leaves on it. And it's the same with the believer in the Savior of the world.

When Jesus came to earth, He performed miracles, signs, and wonders as proof that He was the Son of God. He didn't mince words or make excuses. He did what the Father sent Him to do.

As believers in the One who healed the lame man, shouldn't we give evidence of our relationship with the Healer? Right before ascending back to heaven, Jesus gave the great commission in Mark 16:15-18. " He said to them, "Go into all the world and preach the gospel to all creation. Whoever believes and is baptized will be saved, but whoever does not believe will be condemned. **And these signs will accompany those who believe:** In my name they will drive out demons; they will speak in new tongues; they will pick up snakes with their hands; and when they drink deadly poison, it will not hurt them at all; they will place their hands on sick people, and they will get well." Most churches give only the first part of this passage. But the charge includes all of it.

Most people won't believe unless they see. How will they see, if we don't perform what Jesus said that we would? Are we making Christ out to be a liar because we can't believe Him for it?

163

The ball is in our court. Right before giving up the ghost and dying on the Cross, Jesus said, "it is finished." What did He mean by that?

He meant that the work of Salvation was finished. That included the past, in that present moment, and for all eternity. Jesus went back in time to save as well as He moved into the future and took away all sin, cancelling all debt associated with it. He nailed it all to the Cross. When He got up out of the grave, it was just another sign of His deity.

Even in getting up out of the grave, He left signs with those alive at that time. Over the 40 days after His resurrection, He appeared before 500 people at one time, according to Paul's account written in 1 Corinthians 15:3-6.

God always has witnesses that will testify about who He is. The question today is, will the believers in Jesus the Christ stand up and show some sign of what they believe in?

As you will note, Jesus did not say, "these signs will follow the Pastors, Bishops or Pope." No. He said that these signs will follow *the believer*. That means a newly baptized believer can believe that Jesus will perform miracles *through* them and it's their faith that brings it to pass.

"Without faith it is impossible to please God, because anyone who comes to him must believe that he exists and that he rewards those who earnestly seek him" (Hebrews 11:6 NIV) Don't get it twisted. The working of miracles is an act of God that He works through us by our faith in Him, but He needs a submitted vessel that He can use.

In this section of the Master class, we will explore the five signs that Jesus outlined in Mark 16:15-18 so that you understand the depth of our calling. We are called to be salt and light. Salt flavors food so that it's not bland, but tasty. Salt also preserves meat. Light gives direction and that light is Jesus. That means we are to flavor the world with the Light of Jesus. Come with me as we discover what's next.

164

THE FIRST SIGN OF A BELIEVER

"In my name, they will cast out demons," Mark 16:17

Why would we need to cast out devils, you may ask? It's because demons are on earth to prevent us from knowing Jesus as our Savior. We must not only believe that God exists but so does Satan. He was the angel formerly known as Lucifer and he was once the head of the angelic choir in heaven. Instruments made up his body and as he walked music would play. He brought much joy to God, until he got the bright idea that everyone should worship him instead of God.

Because of this, God threw him and his followers out of heaven, banishing him to the fiery pit of hell. But when Satan encountered Eve in the garden, he was given legal right to rule because man gave it to him through our sinful nature. That's the reason Jesus had to save us. We had no one else that could do it for us. Jesus's life, death, burial, and resurrection reconciled us to God. By the acts of one man, Adam, Satan became a ruler, but by the acts of one man, Jesus, Satan was dethroned. That means that Jesus is now King of all Kings and He's given us the keys to the kingdom of heaven and whatever we bind on earth, is also bound in heaven and whatever we loose on earth is also loosed in heaven. This is significant because we now have authority over Satan and he doesn't like it. He works night and day to keep us distracted from getting to Jesus. That's the reason demons infect people--to manipulate, cause confusion, and deny that God as well as Jesus exists.

So, what do we do when we encounter someone that is demon possessed? We don't need to entertain it or be afraid of it. We take authority over it in Jesus's name. **You are NOT to lay hands on the demon possessed** but you are to cast it out by using your words of authority and the name of Jesus..

165

JESUS CAST OUT DEMONS

"For our struggle is not against flesh and blood, but against the rulers, against the powers, against the world forces of this darkness, against the spiritual forces of wickedness in the heavenly places." Ephesians 6:12. The following are examples of Jesus casting out demons and sending His disciples to do so as well.

1

"And He went into their synagogues preaching throughout Galilee and casting out the demons."

MARK 1:39

2

"And He appointed twelve, so that they would be with Him and that He could send them out to preach, and to have authority to cast out the demons." This authority is a part of the dominion that we exercise as believers in Jesus as the Christ the Son of the living God.

MARK 3:14-15

3

"Behold, I have given you authority to walk on snakes and scorpions, and authority over all the power of the enemy, and nothing will injure you."

LUKE 10:19

4

"Now when evening came, they brought to Him many who were demon-possessed; and He cast out the spirits with a word, and healed all who were ill." Jesus didn't lay hands on the demon-possessed. The laying on of hands causes a transference and you do not want the demons to transfer to you by laying hands on them. Jesus only laid hands on the sick.

MATTHEW 8:16

166

JESUS CAST OUT DEMONS

"For our struggle is not against flesh and blood, but against the rulers, against the powers, against the world forces of this darkness, against the spiritual forces of wickedness in the heavenly places." Ephesians 6:12. The following are examples of Jesus casting out demons and sending His disciples to do so as well.

5

"And as they were going out, behold, a demon-possessed man who was unable to speak was brought to Him. And after the demon was cast out, the man who was previously unable to speak talked; and the crowds were amazed, and were saying, "Nothing like this has ever been seen in Israel." But the Pharisees were saying, "He casts out demons by the ruler of the demons."
MATTHEW 9:32-34

6

""He called His twelve disciples to Him and gave them authority over unclean spirits, to cast them out, and to heal all kinds of sickness and all kinds of disease." Jesus preceded healing by casting out unclean spirits. There's a connection between demon possession and sickness. Unforgiveness is an open door for demons to take possession of believers.

MATTHEW 10:1

7

Jesus's authenticity is questioned by the Pharisees. "Then one possessed with a demon was brought to Him, blind and mute, and He healed him so that the blind and mute man both spoke and saw. When the Pharisees heard it, they said, 'This Man does not cast out demons, except by Beelzebub the ruler of the demons.' (Read entire passage - "strong man")
MATTHEW 12:22-30

8

"Heal the sick, cleanse the lepers, raise the dead, and cast out demons. Freely you have received, freely give."

MATTHEW 10:8

167

JESUS CAST OUT DEMONS

"For our struggle is not against flesh and blood, but against the rulers, against the powers, against the world forces of this darkness, against the spiritual forces of wickedness in the heavenly places." Ephesians 6:12. The following are examples of Jesus casting out demons and sending His disciples to do so as well.

9

"The disciple is not above his teacher, nor the servant above his master. It is enough for the disciple that he be like his teacher and the servant like his master. If they have called the master of the house Beelzebub, how much more will they call those of his household?"

MATTHEW 10:24-25

10

The 7 sons of Sceva, who were Jewish exorcists, tried to cast out demons in the name of Jesus that "Paul preached" out of a man. Verse 16 says, "And the man in whom was the evil spirit, pounced on them and subdued all of them and overpowered them, so that they fled out of that house naked and wounded."

ACTS 19:13-20

11

"John said to Him, "Teacher, we saw someone casting out demons in Your name, and we tried to prevent him because he was not following us." But Jesus said, "Do not hinder him, for there is no one who will perform a miracle in My name, and be able soon afterward to speak evil of Me. For the one who is not against us is for us."

MARK 9:38-40

12

Jesus rebuked the demons in a man's epileptic son because His disciples weren't able to. Jesus said to the disciples that it was their unbelief that kept them from performing that miracle. All it takes is faith the size of a grain of mustard seed to move mountains. "And nothing will be impossible for you. But this kind does not go out except by prayer and fasting."

MATTHEW 17:14-21

JESUS CAST OUT DEMONS

"For our struggle is not against flesh and blood, but against the rulers, against the powers, against the world forces of this darkness, against the spiritual forces of wickedness in the heavenly places." Ephesians 6:12. The following are examples of Jesus casting out demons and sending His disciples to do so as well.

13

"So they went out and preached that men should repent. And they cast out many demons and anointed with oil many who were sick and healed them."

MARK 6:12-13

14

Jesus cast out demons from a man, who was possessed by legions of demons and sent them into a herd of pigs. The herdsmen of those pigs asked Jesus to leave because they were afraid.

LUKE 8:27-37 (ALSO MARK 5:2-17)

15

"The crowds were paying attention to what was being said by Philip, as they heard and saw the signs which he was performing. For in the case of many who had unclean spirits, they were coming out of them shouting with a loud voice; and many who had been paralyzed or limped on crutches were healed. So there was much rejoicing in that city.

ACTS 8:6-8

16

This scripture makes it very clear that casting out demons is a responsibility that every believer possesses. Jesus never went looking for demons, and neither should we. But when they appear, we are to act as Jesus would act — taking authority over them and kicking them out of the lives of believers, and setting the captives free from demonic control.

MARK 16:17

DELIVERANCE

"When a strong *man*, fully armed, guards his own house, his possessions are secure. But when *someone* stronger than he attacks him and overpowers him, *that man* takes away his armor on which he had relied and distributes his plunder. The one who is not with Me is against Me; and the one who does not gather with Me scatters. "When the unclean spirit comes out of a person, it passes through waterless places seeking rest, and not finding *any*, it then says, 'I will return to my house from which I came.' And when it comes, it finds it swept and put in order. Then it goes and brings along seven other spirits more evil than itself, and they come in and live there; and the last *condition* of that person becomes worse than the first." Luke 11:21-26

DELIVERANCE BEGINS AT HOME

Be certain to remove all evil items in your possession that have been tied to occult practices, idol worship or incantations. Many times, this includes games played on PlayStation. You can't deliver someone else until you've been set free first.

WHEN STARTING OUT, DON'T PRACTICE ALONE

Jesus sent 72 people out in pairs for a reason. Demons would love to destroy you because after they pulverize you, you'll never attempt doing it again. Ministry should be in groups.

YOUR AUTHORITY IS IN THE NAME OF JESUS

Rest assured that Jesus is with you and rely on Holy Spirit to guide you as you minister freedom to those held captive by demonic forces.

ENCOUNTERING DEMONS

Can you recall an instance where you encountered an individual whom you believed was possessed by demons? If so, how did you respond when confronted by a satanic entity speaking through another person?

AUTHORITY OVER DEMONS

Have you ever cast out demons by taking authority over them and commanding them to leave that person's body? If so, what happened? If no, why not?

DEMONIC OBJECTS

Have you ever considered objects, such as idols, symbols used in witchcraft or occult practices as a part of freedom from demon possession? How does this knowledge affect your view of the objects you have in your home right now?

170

MY PRAYER TODAY:

Lord give me the strength and courage to take authority over demons. Your Word declares that You have granted me the power over all unclean spirits. I employ this power and deliver those who are entrapped in the grasp of Satan. May your divine light illuminate my path and guide me in my ministry to those who require freedom from the enemy's chokehold, that they may experience complete freedom. I offer this prayer in the name of Jesus. Amen.

MY CONFESSION:

With the power given to me by Jesus, I boldly confess that I have authority over all evil spirits. I have no reason to fear them. Jesus gave me power over all the works of Satan. When I am confronted with a demon, I speak to it, take authority over it, and cast it out in Jesus' name! This declaration is made with unwavering faith in Jesus' holy name. Amen.

NOTES

SECOND SIGN OF A BELIEVER

"They will speak with new tongues."
Mark 16:17

You may ask, what does it mean to "speak with new tongues?" It means exactly what it said. We will speak in new and different kinds of languages that we have not been taught. That can include heavenly as well as earthbound languages.

On the day of Pentecost (Acts 2), right after being filled with the Holy Spirit, not just the Apostles, but all that received the Spirit on that day, spoke in other languages. It was so notable that the crowd of people from every surrounding nation, heard the message spoken in their own language from foreigners and most were from Galilee. It was a sign for the unbelieving listeners to draw to the message due to it's supernatural occurrence. There was no way they could've done it without God.

When speaking in tongues with other believers, it is necessary that there is interpretation of what the message is to the Body. Paul deals with this subject in 1 Corinthians 12 and 14 in regards to speaking in tongues in the presence of other believers. Speaking in tongues, in this instance should edify the Body and is a sign that the Spirit is using this person to deliver it but that same Spirit will also provide interpretation of the message so that the entire Body is edified. There are times when you will pray or sing in tongues and because this is personal to God, He doesn't need interpretation.

With any gift that is dispersed to us by the Spirit of God, get an understanding from the Spirit as to how you are to effectively use it. In every instance, the Holy Spirit will lead you to all Truth.

173

BIBLICAL EXAMPLES

"So, then faith comes by hearing, and hearing by the word of God." Romans 10:17

1

ACTS 2:4

"And they were all filled with the Holy Spirit and began to speak in other tongues as the Spirit gave them utterance."

2

1 CORINTHIANS 14:2

"For one who speaks in a tongue speaks not to men but to God; for no one understands him, but he utters mysteries in the Spirit."

3

1 CORINTHIANS 14:23

"If, therefore, the whole church comes together and all speak in tongues, and outsiders or unbelievers enter, will they not say that you are out of your minds?"

4

ACTS 19:6

"And when Paul had laid his hands on them, the Holy Spirit came on them, and they began speaking in tongues and prophesying."

5

1 CORINTHIANS 12:10

"To another the working of miracles, to another prophecy, to another the ability to distinguish between spirits, to another various kinds of tongues, to another the interpretation of tongues."

6

1 CORINTHIANS 14:13-14

"Therefore, one who speaks in a tongue should pray for the power to interpret. For if I pray in a tongue, my spirit prays but my mind is unfruitful."

174

BIBLICAL EXAMPLES

"So, then faith comes by hearing, and hearing by the word of God." Romans 10:17

7

1 CORINTHIANS 14:22

"Thus tongues are a sign not for believers but for unbelievers, while prophecy is a sign not for unbelievers but for believers."

8

1 CORINTHIANS 14:27

"If any speak in a tongue, let there be only two or at most three, and each in turn, and let someone interpret."

9

1 CORINTHIANS 14:4

"The one who speaks in a tongue builds up himself, but the one who prophesies builds up the church."

10

ACTS 2:11

"Both Jews and proselytes, Cretans and Arabians—we hear them telling in our own tongues the mighty works of God."

11

JUDE 1:20

"But you, beloved, building yourselves up in your most holy faith and praying in the Holy Spirit."

12

ROMANS 8:26

"Likewise the Spirit helps us in our weakness. For we do not know what to pray for as we ought, but the Spirit himself intercedes for us with groanings too deep for words."

175

DISCUSSION POINTS

This process is not complicated or spooky. It's necessary to exercise these spiritual gifts that we've been given so that just like the well trained athlete, we can go the distance. Read and answer the following questions. Be transparent.

HOLY SPIRIT

Have you received the Holy Spirit with evidence of speaking in tongues? If not, what is stopping you from experiencing it today?

1

INDWELLING OF HOLY SPIRIT

If you have been filled with the Spirit and spoken in tongues, what greater manifestation of power or revelation have you experienced?

2

BUILDING THE CHURCH

How does speaking in tongues and interpretation of tongues contribute to the growth and harmony of the church? Furthermore, how can believers ensure that their personal growth does not come at the expense of the church's development?

3

PRAYING IN THE SPIRIT

How often do you take the time to pray in the Spirit? When you do, how much time do you devote to praying in other tongues?

4

176

MY PRAYER TODAY:

Dear Lord, I am grateful for the Holy Spirit's presence in my life, which empowers me to pray and praise You in a supernatural language. My spirit longs to communicate with You, and my ability to do so is enhanced through the gift of speaking in unknown tongues. My mind is limited, and I often struggle to express myself to You. However, through praying and praising in the Spirit, I know that I am communicating with You perfectly and at the highest level. Thank You for this incredible blessing. I desire to use my innermost being to pray, praise, and worship You with all that I have. This is my prayer, in Jesus's Name. Amen.

MY CONFESSION:

I openly declare that I am filled with the Spirit of God and I pray in the Spirit. When I was baptized in the Holy Spirit, God empowered me to communicate with Him in a supernatural language. I will not overlook, dismiss or refuse to use this gift from God, and I make it a habit to pray in tongues frequently. This practice has enabled me to grow stronger and more receptive to the workings of the Holy Spirit, resulting in a constant flow of supernatural activity manifesting in my life. I declare this in Jesus's Name. Amen.

NOTES

THIRD SIGN OF A BELIEVER

"They will pick up serpents"
Mark 16:18

Eek! Snakes give me the heebie-jeebies. I don't know about you, but I am terrified of snakes. But hold up. Did Jesus really want us to start catching snakes? If so, does that mean that I'm not a believer because I won't do it?

Absolutely not. Jesus was again speaking of the signs that will point unbelievers to Him. Everyone knows that if a snake bites you and you don't receive medical help, you will die. But when we see someone take up a snake out of **necessity** because of impending danger to oneself or others, and they don't die from lack of medical attention, we know God protected them by His supernatural power. Those poisonous stings from snakes become null and void.

But if you look at this statement more broadly, you will see that the serpent symbolizes Satan. Satan is the serpent that believers can take up without being harmed. That is the immunity we have against the serpent for all who believe in Jesus as their Savior. This "taking up serpents" in regard to Satan involves Jesus's statements made in Luke 10:19, "Behold, I give unto you power to tread on serpents and scorpions, and over all the power of the enemy: and nothing shall by any means hurt you."

On the following pages, we will take a look at scripture references that show those that encountered snakes and how they fared.

179

BIBLICAL EXAMPLES

The keys to harnessing your fears is to build your faith in Jesus and faith comes by hearing biblical as well as current testimonies of witnesses to God's power to save from the snare of serpents.

NUMBERS 21:6-9

" Then the Lord sent venomous snakes among them; they bit the people and many Israelites died. The people came to Moses and said, "We sinned when we spoke against the Lord and against you. Pray that the Lord will take the snakes away from us." So Moses prayed for the people. The Lord said to Moses, "Make a snake and put it up on a pole; anyone who is bitten can look at it and live." So Moses made a bronze snake and put it up on a pole. Then when anyone was bitten by a snake and looked at the bronze snake, they lived.

ACTS 28:3-6

Paul gathered a pile of brushwood and, as he put it on the fire, a viper, driven out by the heat, fastened itself on his hand. When the islanders saw the snake hanging from his hand, they said to each other, "This man must be a murderer; for though he escaped from the sea, the goddess Justice has not allowed him to live." But Paul shook the snake off into the fire and suffered no ill effects. The people expected him to swell up or suddenly fall dead; but after waiting a long time and seeing nothing unusual happen to him, they changed their minds and said he was a god."

MATTHEW 23:33

"ye serpents, ye generation of vipers, how can ye escape the damnation of hell." Those who believe in Christ are empowered to rule over the serpent without fear of harm. For non-believers, Satan has dominion over them as he is the great deceiver who comes to steal, kill, and destroy. Non-believers are like slaves to Satan, where he holds sin like the power of death over them. However, for believers, Satan is a defeated foe whom Christ freed all believers from being slaves to sin. For us, this serpent has no power to harm us as Christ removed Satan's fangs, rendering him powerless over us.

GOING DEEPER

From the scripture references above and from your own experiences, please read the following questions and answer to the best of your knowledge.

ONE
Do you know someone who was supernaturally protected by the power of God when something catastrophic happened, but it had no effect on them?

TWO
How does the image of handling snakes align with the broader message that we possess a supernatural immunity against the serpent, representing Satan?

THREE
How does the insight from Luke 10:19 challenge and deepen our understanding of spiritual warfare and the protection we get through our faith in Jesus?

FOUR
How do these instances contribute to your understanding of God's protection and the role of faith?

FIVE
How can taking up snakes be seen as an act of faith in the face of danger, and what implications does this have for you navigating challenges and threats in your spiritual journey?

SIX
Considering fear of snakes, how does the call to take up snakes as a sign serve as a powerful metaphor for confronting and overcoming the influence of Satan in one's life?

SEVEN
In what ways can you translate this symbolic act into practical and tangible expressions of faith, resilience, and victory over the spiritual adversaries you encounter?

181

MY PRAYER TODAY:

Dear Heavenly Father, I absolutely and unequivocally trust in the truth of Your Word. I declare with faith that no harm can befall me while I am doing the work that you sent me to do and as I share Your message with people in new and unfamiliar places. Your promise of divine protection fills me with gratitude and confidence, knowing that Your strength shields me from all that may seek to harm me. Thank You, Jesus for your unwavering love and protection. This is my prayer, in Jesus's Name. Amen.

MY CONFESSION:

I declare God is my Shield and my fortress. Therefore, I'm shielded from any harm that comes my way. Whether I experience impending dangers while driving on dangerous roads, ministering in remote or risky areas of the world, I know I'm always safe. I trust God's power to save me, knowing that He's got my back and will guide me through every step of the journey. So, no matter the challenges I face, I will not fear because with faith in my heart and Jesus always with me, I'm unstoppable. This is my declaration in Jesus's name. Amen!

NOTES

FOURTH SIGN OF A BELIEVER

"... and if they drink any deadly poison, it will not harm them "
Mark 16:18

This portion of what Jesus said trips a lot of people up. Jesus is not commanding us to consume deadly poison. But I believe that if a believer in Jesus accidentally drinks anything poisonous that would normally kill someone, they will not die from it.

Remember this verse is dealing with the Great Commission to take the Gospel throughout the world. This verse is a continuation of that Great Commission. Jesus is not idly speaking of our everyday activities, unless your everyday activity is to carry the Gospel to those in need of it. He is speaking of the mission and in so doing, it guarantees our safety while doing God's work.

All of these words of comfort that Jesus spoke before leaving earth was His own declaration that further seals that He will never leave or forsake us. We can rest assured that whatever schemes or tricks that Satan uses to snare us, even deadly poison, to try to stop our assignments that they won't work because we have supernatural intervention. It's the year of the Lord's favor as prescribed in Isaiah 61. All of heaven is backing us up as we complete our assignments, "to proclaim the good news to the poor; to bind up the brokenhearted; to proclaim freedom for the captive of sin and release from darkness for the prisoners. It's our job to proclaim the year of the Lord's favor and the day of vengeance of God, to comfort all who mourn, and provide for those who grieve in Zion--to bestow on them a crown of beauty instead of ashes, the oil of joy instead of mourning, and a garment of praise instead of a spirit of despair."

Jesus, with His final words, is assuring us that the same resurrection power that raised him from the dead is keeping us from all harm that the enemy would try to use against us. 184

DISCUSSION POINTS

In light of the potential interference that Satan will try to use against us, Jesus offers reassurance that no harm will befall us. Read the following questions and answer them to the best of your knowledge and understanding.

Considering Jesus's assurance that believers will not be harmed by deadly poison as they fulfill the Great Commission, how does this promise influence the mindset and actions of those engaged in spreading the Gospel?

In what ways does this supernatural intervention described in this context offer us a sense of security and embolden us to carry out the mission, especially in the face of potential dangers, and how can this assurance impact our approach to evangelism and spreading the message of hope?

MY PRAYER TODAY:

Dear Lord, I am grateful for the courage You have given me to follow Your path. Thank you for being my Rock, my shield, and my strong tower. I refuse to be afraid, intimidated, or held back, and I have faith in You, that wherever I go You are with me. Holy Spirit, please empower me and grant me clarity of thought to make wise decisions. The harvest is plentiful and I know that as you send me out to do your work, You supernaturally protect me everywhere that I go. Thank You for Your guidance and support. I pray this in Jesus' name, Amen.

MY CONFESSION:

I decree and declare that my body is immune to all harmful substances because of the Blood of Jesus. With the Holy Spirit living in me, I'm protected from all kinds of evil like scorpions, snakes, poison, and all other works of the enemy. God promised me a safe and smooth journey as I do the work of ministry, with no room for worry or injustice. I reject any feelings of fear and instead embrace the supernatural life of Jesus Christ. I affirm this with unwavering faith in the name of Jesus. Amen.

NOTES

I believe.

FIFTH SIGN OF A BELIEVER

"they will lay hands on the sick, and they will recover."
Mark 16:18

I remember the first time I felt a lump in my breast. I prayed over that lump for months. I was desperate. I needed God to prove to me that He is a healer for *me*. Not just those people written on the pages of my bible. I needed the Healer that lives in me to show the world through me that He heals. It's not that medicine can't work. I needed a miracle.

I also remember the day, months later, when I went to pray over that same lump, and as I prayed, I felt the lump dissolve. Hallelujah! It was gone. But then another one appeared and with each occurrence, my faith in God's power to perform grew, until one time, I found a lump, prayed, and it dissolved on the same day. At that point, my faith in God was unwavering.

What about you? Do you pray to God, believing that He will heal you? God will always answer. No matter whether it's a healing on this side of life or in the life to come, He will come through for you when you believe in Him. Sometimes we have to wait for God to answer but they that wait on God will not be put to shame.

Just as doctors practice medicine, we must practice or exercise the gift of healing that we've been given. It's not automatic because faith in God is an essential part of the healing process. Faith grows with time and experience and in experiencing God, our knowledge and authority increases.

Rest assured that with the same intention that God chose you, He will perfect the gifts that He has placed in you and His words will never return to Him void. He will finish what He began in you.

188

BIBLICAL EXAMPLES

There are many pastors and church leaders that do not believe that this scripture is for us. But Jesus said He will heal the sick through us. The following are examples of the apostles laying hands on and praying for the sick. Let's discover through the written word their stories of healing through the name of Jesus.

"And they took offense at Him. But Jesus said to them, "A prophet is not dishonored except in his own hometown and in his own household." **And He did not do many miracles there because of their unbelief**."

MATTHEW 13:57-58; MARK 6:4-13

"...Peter, along with John, looked straight at him and said, "Look at us." So he turned to them, expecting to get something from them. But Peter said, "I don't have silver or gold, but what I do have, I give you: In the name of Jesus Christ of Nazareth, get up and walk!" Then, taking him by the right hand he raised him up, and at once his feet and ankles became strong."

ACTS 3:1-7 (CSB)

"As a result, they would carry the sick out into the streets and lay them on cots and mats so that when Peter came by, at least his shadow might fall on some of them. In addition, a multitude came together from the towns surrounding Jerusalem, bringing the sick and those who were tormented by unclean spirits, and they were all healed."

ACTS 5:12-16 (CSB)

"There he found a man named Aeneas, who was paralyzed and had been bedridden for eight years. Peter said to him, "Aeneas, Jesus Christ heals you. Get up and make your bed," and immediately he got up."

ACTS 9:32-34 (CSB)

BIBLICAL EXAMPLES

There are many pastors and church leaders that do not believe that this scripture is for us. But Jesus said He will heal the sick through us. The following are examples of the apostles laying hands on and praying for the sick. Let's discover through the written word their stories of healing through the name of Jesus.

"In Lystra a man was sitting who was without strength in his feet, had never walked, and had been lame from birth. He listened as Paul spoke. After looking directly at him and seeing that he had faith to be healed, Paul said in a loud voice, "Stand up on your feet!" And he jumped up and began to walk around."

ACTS 14:8-10 (CSB)

"...As she followed Paul and us she cried out, "These men, who are proclaiming to you the way of salvation, are the servants of the Most High God." She did this for many days. Paul was greatly annoyed. Turning to the spirit, he said, "I command you in the name of Jesus Christ to come out of her!" And it came out right away."

ACTS 16:16-18 (CSB)

"This went on for two years, so that all the residents of Asia, both Jews and Greeks, heard the word of the Lord. God was performing extraordinary miracles by Paul's hands, so that even facecloths or aprons that had touched his skin were brought to the sick, and the diseases left them, and the evil spirits came out of them."

ACTS 19:10-12 (CSB)

"Publius's father was in bed suffering from fever and dysentery. Paul went to him, and praying and laying his hands on him, he healed him."

ACTS 28:8 (CSB)

MY PRAYER TODAY:

Dear Lord, I humbly come to you asking for the boldness and confidence to lay my hands on the sick so that the world will know that You still perform miracles. I ask that your healing power flows through me and into the bodies of those who are battling illness, that it may combat the enemy's work and restore them to good health. Your Word says that believers can heal the sick by laying their hands on them, and I choose to act on that today. I believe in You and I will place my hands on the sick, praying so that your healing power may be delivered through me to others. I make this declaration in the name of Jesus, the only Healer. Amen.

MY CONFESSION:

I have faith that God's power is activated when I lay my hands on those afflicted with illnesses. Just as medicine reverses a medical condition, God's supernatural power is transferred when I place my hands on the sick and it reverses the diagnosis, restoring them to good health. I boldly declare that I will lay hands on the sick, just as Jesus did when He was ministering on earth. I am confident that they will be healed, and I declare this with unwavering faith in Jesus's name. Amen.

191

NOTES

SIGNS OF A BELIVER

KEY TAKEAWAYS

- They will cast out demons.
- They will speak with new languages.
- They will pick up serpents.
- If they drink deadly poison, and it will not harm them.
- They will lay hands on the sick and they will recover.

It takes courage to have faith in the words that Jesus spoke in Mark 16:17-19, when even church leaders and pastors don't believe. I think it's an important fact that these were some of the last words spoken by Jesus before ascending back to heaven.

It is His expectation that we will follow Him and do what He said. If you believe that the bible is the infallible Word of God, how can you not believe these instructions? God is the same yesterday, today, and forevermore. If Jesus healed the sick, the lame, and those stricken with schizophrenia back then, he will most certainly continue to heal them through His Holy Spirit working in us.

What is most important is that you do what Jesus said do and He will be the one to perform miracles as a sign that we belong to Him. Every act that we participate with God in points back to Jesus as the Savior of the world. These are only signs so that the world believes in Him--not us.

SECTION 6: THE GREATER WORKS

THE GREATER WORKS

"WHOEVER BELIEVES IN ME WILL DO THE WORKS I HAVE BEEN DOING, AND THEY WILL DO EVEN GREATER THINGS THAN THESE, BECAUSE I AM GOING TO THE FATHER."

- JOHN 14:12

THE GREATER WORKS

ARE YOU SERIOUS?

What is Jesus saying? Does He really mean that you and I, as believers in Him, will do greater things than He did? Absolutely He does. But Jesus walked on water, turned water into wine, fed 5000 with only two fish and five loaves of bread. He healed the lame man and with just a touch, the bleeding dried up for a woman that was on her period for twelve years. You mean to tell me, we will do something like that? That's what Jesus said and that's what He meant.

But how? By faith. Faith is the *substance* of things hoped for and the *evidence* of things not yet realized or manifested. Faith in what? That God will do what He said He will do through us. Miracles are not about us. It's about the One who sent us.

If Jesus is still alive in us, why wouldn't He do what the Father sent Him to do--even through a black woman raised in Georgia? Can we believe Jesus for salvation but not for the greater works?

Read chapter 12: The Crossing in "Bulletproof" companion book.

197

" For the Father loves the Son and shows him all he does. Yes, and he will show him even greater works than these, so that you will be amazed." John 5:20

"BY FAITH, WE WERE IN THE ROOM WHEN JESUS GAVE THAT CHARGE."

- LAURAINE WHITE

As I began writing this chapter, I paused because I was thinking about what people are going to say about what I've written in these pages. I grappled with the notion long enough, then I went to my computer. I googled "the greater works" and what I found was appalling.

Well educated and renowned men and women of the cloth have written that Jesus didn't mean that we would perform miracles, as He did, but we would do other works of ministry. They purported that no one can do miracles but Jesus, *and **they are right***. But we are not claiming that we can do miracles on our own. We are only the conduit or pass through for the Spirit to do the greater works.

During that night, I tossed, turned, and wrestled with the things my imagination contrived about what the religious will have to say. Then I was awakened by the Spirit at 3 am. I was in tears because all I want to do is rightly divide the Truth to those seeking it. So, I bore my soul to the Spirit of God and He reassured me that those were His Words to us. He didn't say it only to those in the room at that time.

By faith, we were in that room when He gave that charge. You were on His mind when He said it. He chose you to do great works, not for a show or to boast. No. It was to demonstrate that the power of God is still at work in mere mortals. Only God can do such a thing.

During that same night, the Spirit of God took me back down memory lane. He reminded me about how He ordered my steps over the last 20+ years. Of how it was divinely set up for me to walk closely with two great men of God that I witnessed with my own eyes perform great miracles--legitimately. It wasn't by accident, but was orchestrated by divine means to reframe my thinking. He reminded me how it was His Spirit that I felt like a wind blow on me. He didn't just do it to have something to do. No. It was with a purpose that He drew me to Himself.

198

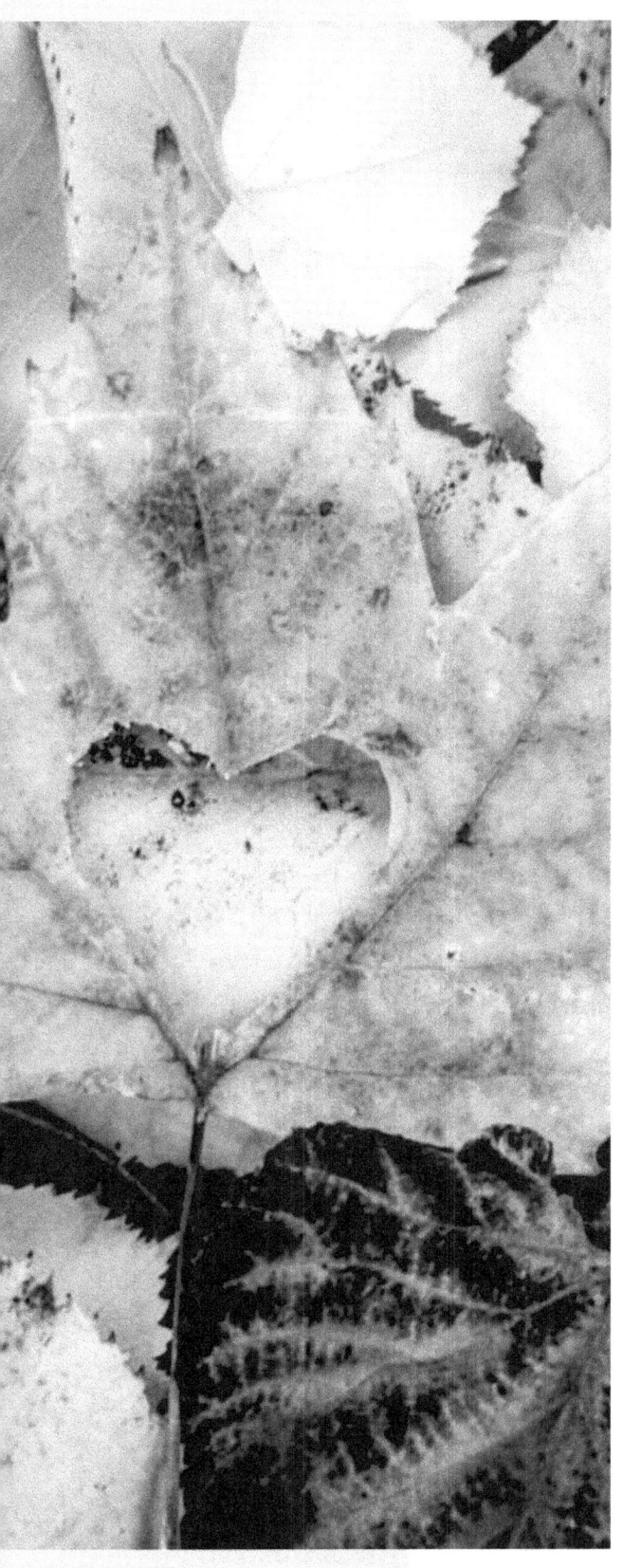

God blew on me so that I was equipped to do the work that he called me to do. He wasn't going to call me to do it without giving me His Spirit to perfect the work. In this flesh of mine dwells no good thing, but when the Lord blew on me, I was never the same again. As I write this, I'm humbled to know that I was a part of God's plan. He wanted to use someone of low estate like me to do His work. That's priceless.

He wanted it to be obvious that I am not able to do any of the things He does through me. Therefore, those that witness the miracles wrought through me are compelled to believe in Jesus. Because of my imperfections, He is glorified.

He took me back in time to recall how I saw with my own eyes a man come into one of our services in a wheelchair because he had Multiple Sclerosis but walked on his own two legs out of the services when it was over. He came in contact with the healing power of Jesus and was delivered. Hallelujah!

We watched miracle after miracle every week because *God* was at work in us. It wasn't just our Bishop laying hands, but we had teams of people laying hands as evidence that **Jesus** is still the Healer. Then beyond laying hands, everyone prayed believing that God would heal and He did.

IF
NOT
NOW
WHEN?

AN INVITATION

That's why I am here. I'm not just here to testify about what God has done for me, but that through my story you will be compelled to hear what God has for you. I want to invite you to participate with God to do the greater works that He wants to do through you. It's not by accident that you are reading and/or participating in this course. God ordered your steps to this material for such a time as this.

All hell broke through on my life to try to stop me from doing this work, but as I'm finishing this Master class, I'm already seeing signs of the promised restoration that God gave to me at the time He blew on me. That's how I know. God has a strategic plan with you in mind and it won't work without you.

God's calling you. Won't you answer Him with a yes? Today, you must make a decision, whether you've pondered it before or not. Today is your day to open your heart to become what God planned for you to become. This is your time. Walk into it.

YOU+JESUS=GREATER WORKS

In this next portion, we will delve into some of the miracles of Jesus. We will observe and discuss the nature of the problem, whether it was an illness or demon possession to understand the path that Jesus took to deliver each of these people during His time on earth. Stay open to hear what the Spirit of God is speaking to you. He is sealing His work in you through these discussions.

THE GREATER WORKS

"Jesus did many other things as well. If every one of them was written down, I suppose that even the whole world would not have room for the books that would be written." John 21:25

- Jesus changed water into wine (John 2:1-11).

- Jesus cured the nobleman's son (John 4:46-47).

- The great haul of fishes (Luke 5:1-11).

- Jesus cast out an unclean spirit (Mark 1:23-28).

- Jesus cured Peter's mother-in-law of a fever (Mark 1:30-31).

- Jesus healed a leper (Mark 1:40-45).

- Jesus healed the centurion's servant (Matthew 8:5-13).

- Jesus raised the widow's son from the dead (Luke 7:11-18).

- Jesus stilled the storm (Matthew 8:23-27).

- Jesus cured two demon-possessed (Matthew 8:28-34).

- Jesus cured the paralytic (Matthew 9:1-8).

- Jesus raised the ruler's daughter from the dead (Matthew 9:18-26).

- Jesus cured a woman of an issue of blood (Luke 8:43-48).

- Jesus opened the eyes of two blind men (Matthew 9:27-31).

- Jesus loosened the tongue of a man who could not speak (Matthew 9:32-33).

- Jesus healed an invalid man at the pool called Bethesda (John 5:1-9).

- Jesus restored a withered hand (Matthew 12:10-13).

- Jesus cured a demon-possessed man (Matthew 12:22).

THE GREATER WORKS

"Jesus did many other things as well. If every one of them was written down, I suppose that even the whole world would not have room for the books that would be written." John 21:25

- Jesus fed at least five thousand people (Matthew 14:15-21).

- Jesus healed a woman of Canaan (Matthew 15:22-28).

- Jesus cured a deaf and mute man (Mark 7:31-37).

- Jesus fed at least four thousand people (Matthew 15:32-39).

- Jesus opened the eyes of a blind man (Mark 8:22-26).

- Jesus cured a boy who was plagued by a demon (Matthew 17:14-21).

- Jesus opened the eyes of a man born blind (John 9:1-38).

- Jesus cured a woman who had been afflicted for eighteen years (Luke 13:10-17).

- Jesus cured a man of dropsy (Luke 14:1-4).

- Jesus healed the woman with the issue of blood for twelve years (Luke 8:43-48).

- Jesus cleansed ten lepers (Luke 17:11-19).

- Jesus raised Lazarus from the dead (John 11:1-46).

- Jesus opened the eyes of two blind men (Matthew 20:30-34).

- Jesus caused the fig tree to wither (Matthew 21:18-22).

- Jesus restored the ear of the high priest's servant (Luke 22:50-51).

- Jesus rose from the dead (Luke 24:5-8).

- The second great haul of fishes (John 21:1-14).

- Even in death, Jesus's miracles continued as the tombs broke open and many holy people that were dead were raised to life, appearing to their families as witnesses of Jesus's power. (Matthew 27:51-53).

START WITH WHY

At this point, you may be asking, "Why me?" Why not you? Jesus chooses the common person to do uncommon things.

The apostles were common, ordinary people until they met Jesus. Their decision to follow Him changed the course of their lives and as a result, changed all of ours. This can happen through you, too. If you're open to being used by God to do His work, He promises to not only back you up while you do the work, but also reward you for doing so.

"Jesus said, "I assure you and most solemnly say to you, there is no one who has given up a house or brothers or sisters or mother or father or children or farms, for My sake and for the gospel's sake, who will not receive a hundred times as much now in the present age—houses and brothers and sisters and mothers and children and farms—along with persecutions; and in the age to come, eternal life. But many who are first will be last, and the last, first."
Mark 10:29-31

203

SECTION 7: WHAT'S NEXT

SECTION 7

WHAT'S NEXT?

SECTION 7

SPIRITUALITY

FAITH LOVE WORSHIP HEAVEN MEDITATION RELIGION CULTURE GOD SPIRIT

UNITY AURA DEVOTION LIGHT NIRVANA PRAYERS PARADISE SOUL BELIEVE

WHAT'S NEXT

Read chapter 3: Twelve in "Bulletproof" companion book.

"But you are not like that, for you are a chosen people. You are royal priests, a holy nation, God's very own possession. As a result, you can show others the goodness of God, for he called you out of the darkness into his wonderful light. "Once you had no identity as a people; now you are God's people. Once you received no mercy; now you have received God's mercy." 1 Peter 2:9-10

Have you ever been so convinced that you were right about something then found out later that you were wrong? I have. I had just moved into a condominium and was assigned two parking spaces that were numbered. Because I was only driving one car at the time, I only needed one parking space.

One day, I came home from work, parked my car, and noticed that there was a car parked next to me. I became livid. Who is this that parked in my assigned parking space? I took a picture of their license plate and the car with the number of the parking space shown in the image. With these pictures, I emailed the manager of the property, immediately, to let them know about the infraction but for three days, I didn't hear back from them.

For three days, I was fuming. The car never moved. Every morning that I left for work and evening that I returned the car was parked in what I perceived to be my assigned parking space. I was fussing every time I went to my car or when I would return home. How dare

"JESUS IS CALLING YOU. WHY WON'T YOU ANSWER?"

- LAURAINE WHITE

they park in my space. I barked about it and felt my blood boil every time I even thought about it. On the third day, I was busy, looking for pen and paper so that I could write a nasty note to them telling them to move their car, but I never found anything in my car.

On the fourth day, I was coming home from the grocery store and noticed that another car was parked on the other side of the car that I thought was parked illegally. When I observed the car parked there, it was not the vehicle of the people that I know normally park next to mine. I began to look again and noticed that I was the one parked in the wrong parking space.

The people that I had parked in their parking space, ended up parking in mine. What would've happened if I had left a nasty note on their car? Can you imagine their reaction to getting that note? They would've laughed and claimed that I was crazy, right? I would have felt like such a fool.

My error here was an easy fix. No harm, no foul, right? But what about your beliefs about Jesus being the Son of God or whether God really

exists? What if, when life is over for all of us, and we find out that Jesus is the Son of God and that there is a judgment that is rendered with hell as the home for those that do not believe, what will be the harm to you? Have you ever thought about that? What is your conclusion?

Are you picking up what I am laying down? Life is hard. The decisions we make on this side of life are vital to where we live in eternity. Oops. That may be another bone of contention for you—that there is a place in eternity for us all. But I believe that with my whole being and I would not hold back that information, even from my enemies. But I am not here to cast judgment. I am here to inform you. I am here to support you.

If I am wrong about Jesus, I have nothing to lose. But if you're wrong, everything is at stake. Are you willing to run the risk, rolling the dice that none of this is accurate?

GOD'S AGENDA

Or maybe you believe in Jesus but you're not sold on the idea that He chose you. What if that's the missing piece and why you feel so lost or empty inside? What if submitting your life to Christ is the only thing that will fill that gaping hole?

What if you are the next Kathryn Kuhlman, Mother Rosa Horn or Aimee Semple McPherson. God used these women to perform great miracles because they dared to believe that God wanted to use them.

Maybe God has called you to be the next William J. Seymour, who initiated the Azusa Street revivals by just holding prayer in the home of Edward Lee on April 9, 1906. The power of God rested on that entire street, such that a revival broke out and continued until 1915. Miracle after miracle was performed by God through this man's faith in God. Or maybe God wants to use you like He used my father in ministry, Bishop Milton Bento Perry. Everywhere he went, God performed miracles and it began when he was just a child.

WHAT'S NEXT

"Jesus looked at them and said, "With man this is impossible, but with God all things are possible." Matthew 19:26

Don't limit God. Who knows what can be accomplished when you connect your gifts and talents with your faith in God. What if you use your gifts of music to thank and worship God? Even if you still want to do other forms of music, you can give a tenth of all your music to God and He will bless the rest of it.

What I'm saying is there's no limit to the possibilities when you put your faith and trust in God. Jesus is the door that you use to enter and He has given you the keys through His Spirit and this training to do what only He can do through you.

That's a great door that is open for you. I've never regretted one day that I've spent with Him and I don't think you will either. Receiving salvation through Jesus and His Holy Spirit insures that stepping into that door holds a whole new world for you.

209

WHAT'S NEXT

"But everyone who hears these words of mine and does not put them into practice is like a foolish man who built his house on sand. The rain came down, the streams rose, and the winds blew and beat against that house, and it fell with a great crash."
Matthew 7:26-27

We're entering a season of uncertainty and it's important that you choose now whose side you're on. As things begin to play out and unfold before us, what looks like it's up today will fall down and you will then be desperate for a Savior. Don't wait for that to happen.

Get up and look at where you are today. From where you stand, things look great. Things are going your way. In your mind's eye, you don't need anyone or anything. You've got this all in the bag, right? You pulled yourself up by your own abilities and intelligence. Those were your ideas. No one else went with you to earn the education, experience, and exposure to be in the room with the movers and shakers that catapulted you to the front of the line. You're doing things and going places that you and your family could only dream of doing, but now that's become your reality.

Look again. Tomorrow is going to look vastly different. Mark my words. The things (not people) that you hold dear will not matter. There's a great shaking happening and in short order, those that have been reckless with their lives will regret it. The extravagance and living on the edge will not pay to get you out of it.

The Word says, "There is a way that seems right to a man, but its end is the way of death." Proverbs 14:12. There's another scripture that says, the wages earned from choosing sin over life in Christ is death or separation from the only Life Source which is Jesus Christ.

BREAKING IT DOWN

You can't see, until you see. Why did we go through all of these exercises? The preparation stages, understanding spiritual weapons, and how they are used? What are we moving toward? Miracles, signs, and wonders? We don't need to see miracles, just to see miracles. There will be a desperate cry for signs and for God to save them.

We are in a time just as the story in Luke 12:16-21 depicts a rich man who earned a windfall with his harvest one year and because of his vast riches, he had the need to tear down what was sufficient for his needs to build larger ones, as evidence of his affluence and power. In all of his accumulation of things, he was totally unprepared for what came next.

The same night that he made up in his mind to tear down what he had to build bigger, he died. Guess where he opened his eyes on the other side of life? In torment. In Hell. That place of agony and there is no relief there.

211

"YOU CAN'T SEE, UNTIL YOU SEE. LOOK BEYOND THE IMMEDIATE AND YOU WILL SEE THE IMPOSSIBLE BECOME POSSIBLE."

- LAURAINE WHITE

WHAT'S NEXT

When Jesus was born, there had been no prophecy for 500 years. God was silent. He chose to not say a word to any man. God shut His mouth and would not speak to a man for 500 years concerning the state of the world. Why is that?

The world had become out of control. It was violent. Even the religious had forgotten God and turned to the ways of the world. They had no regard for God.

Does that sound familiar? Today, violence is at an all-time high. Every major city in the US, the land of the free, deals with an extreme guns and weapons crisis. The prisons are overrun with our children and don't mention the school to prison initiative that has been underway since the 1980's.

Nothing matters to those in power except to keep capitalism going, at all costs. That means you and I are casualties of that war.

213

And don't mention the leaders of the Lord's Church. They look more like the world than ever. They are involved in more drama than the soap operas my mother watched when I was a child. They're more interested in offerings than repentance and they're wrapped up in living baller lifestyles than that of a life consecrated to Jesus. They would rather get in the pulpit to entertain than to teach what God desires for us to hear.

Slipping and dipping in all kinds of foolishness that grieves our Lord and Savior to the point that He must step in and herd His sheep back to Himself. He's disgusted with us.

All of creation is also moaning. We have been having extreme weather patterns that have never happened before. Ice and snow in hot Dallas, TX and temperatures so high in Canada that ice skating rinks melt from the sweltering heat.

It's not because of global warming. It's because we've left God. The Word in 2 Chronicles 7:14 says, "If my people, which are called by my name, shall humble themselves, and pray, and seek my face, and turn from their wicked ways; then will I hear from heaven, and will forgive their sin, and **will heal their land**." God can turn our global warming around with just one word if we would only repent and return to Him.

ANOTHER CHANCE

Why do you think that God is speaking to us now? Why is today any different than it was prior to Jesus's birth? Why is God not silent now? What changed His mind about us? There has to be a very good reason for God to speak now.

BECAUSE
of Love

It's because of Jesus's death, burial, and resurrection. It has to do with Jesus being seated at the right hand of God the Father. He's interceding for us. Jesus is the One that took it all for us and is still fighting for our salvation--not just in eternity, but right here, right now. And He won't let go, even with His own Father. He steps in when God the Father is angry with us and pleads His Blood over our sins.

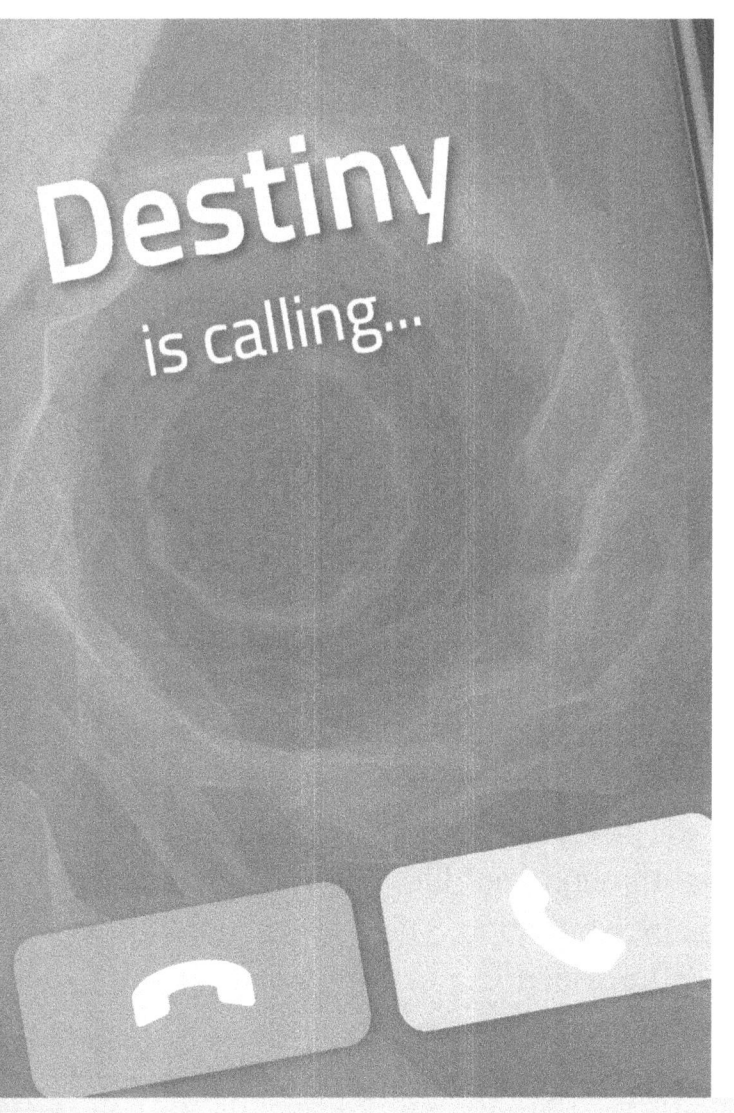

LOVE ENDURES

When God sees us now, He sees the blood of His Son. That's the difference. It's nothing about us. Things didn't change until we decided to accept Jesus as our Savior. Then everything changed.

It was because of love that He came to earth, endured the suffering of the Cross, died, was buried, then was resurrected. For love's sake, He wouldn't come off the Cross because He saw you and me without any chance of being saved and He hung in without complaining.

Not one time did He ever see His suffering as punishment. He saw it as our way out. His suffering had our names written on it.

LOVE WON IT ALL

His love for us wouldn't let Him call down legions of angels to save Him. Jesus saw it through to the end and because He did, we are free to have a relationship with the Father. Jesus's sacrifice moved the Father to adopt us into His royal family. As a part of the Kingdom, will you begin to exercise the authority given to you to reign in the earth? All of creation is groaning in anticipation and excitement as they wait eagerly for the manifestation of the children of God. (Romans 8:19)

The time is now to accept Jesus's call. Don't wait. The world needs the God in you to rise up and do the greater works. Don't allow naysayers to keep you bound to doing nothing. You were born for this. As you accept the call, surrender to the Holy Spirit. He will lead you to do great and marvelous things, if you would dare to believe. It's when you step into this season without reservation that we will see God do amazing things. Let the world see the pages of their bible become real through your life. The following pages give an action plan for when the enemy comes in like a flood. There is a scripture that you can pray for every circumstance and the list provided is a starting point for you to decree over your circumstances so that you live free and maintain dominion.

ACTION PLAN

1

READ 2 CORINTHIANS 10:3-5

Read the Bible regularly so the Holy Spirit can "remind you" of what Scripture says during Satan's attacks.

2

READ JAMES 1:22-25

Be careful to obey scripture in your daily life. It's important that we are not just readers of the word, but also doers of it. Change happens when we make a practical application of the Word .

3

READ 1 PETER 5:8-9

Allow the Holy Spirit to sanctify you and teach you obedience. This happens when we open ourselves to allow the Holy Spirit to live in us, thereby, changing us from the inside out.

4

READ JAMES 4:7

"Resist the devil and he will flee." Resist means to repeal, not to agree with, not to receive his thoughts into your mind and soul and not to entertain anything that is contrary to the Word of God.

5

READ 1 JOHN 1:9, 5:11-13, GALATIANS 2:20-21, JOHN 15:9-12

Quote Scripture back to Satan as Jesus did. Memorize a few key verses for this purpose, such as those listed above, and others as the Holy Spirit instructs you to.

6

READ 1 JOHN 5:4-5

Focus on overcoming the World and Satan. Remember, our fight is not with people. Jesus commanded us to love one another. Satan's job is to divide us so that He keeps control of the world.

7

READ ECCLESIASTES 4:9-12

Unity with other Christians. Make a declaration of interdependence with true "believers" and work together. Satan uses the age-old strategy of "divide and conquer."

ACTION PLAN

"For though we live in the world, we do not wage war as the world does. The weapons we fight with are not the weapons of the world. On the contrary, they have divine power to demolish strongholds. We demolish arguments and every pretension that sets itself up against the knowledge of God, and we take captive every thought to make it obedient to Christ." 2 Corinthians 10:3-5. The following are examples of ways that the world handles disagreements, fights, and/or deals in war efforts.

WORLDLY WEAPONS	
POLITICAL POWERS	ACTS OF TERRORISM
ORGANIZED PROGRAMS	DEMONSTRATIONS
BOYCOTTS	PICKETING
ACTS OF VIOLENCE	ARSON/LOOTING

ACTION PLAN

COMMON PROBLEMS OF THE WORLD		
Depression	Discouragement	Betrayal
Money	Social pressures	Family troubles
Greed	Guilt	Shame
Race Problems	War	Poverty
Air and Water Pollution	Disease	Death
Economy / Inflation	Taxes	Stocks/Bonds/Commodities Market

ACTION PLAN

OUR WEAPONS AGAINST THE PROBLEMS OF THIS WORLD

MATTHEW 18:18 "TRULY I TELL YOU, WHATEVER YOU BIND ON EARTH WILL BE BOUND IN HEAVEN, AND WHATEVER YOU LOOSE ON EARTH WILL BE LOOSED IN HEAVEN.	EPHESIANS 2:6, "AND GOD RAISED US UP WITH CHRIST AND SEATED US WITH HIM IN THE HEAVENLY REALMS IN CHRIST JESUS."
1 CORINTHIANS 6:2-3, "OR DO YOU NOT KNOW THAT THE LORD'S PEOPLE WILL JUDGE THE WORLD? AND IF YOU ARE TO JUDGE THE WORLD, ARE YOU NOT COMPETENT TO JUDGE TRIVIAL CASES? DO YOU NOT KNOW THAT WE WILL JUDGE ANGELS? HOW MUCH MORE THE THINGS OF THIS LIFE!"	PSALM 91:11, "FOR HE WILL COMMAND HIS ANGELS CONCERNING YOU TO GUARD YOU IN ALL YOUR WAYS;"
JOSHUA 23:10, "ONE OF YOUR MEN PUTS TO FLIGHT A THOUSAND, FOR THE LORD YOUR GOD IS HE WHO FIGHTS FOR YOU, JUST AS HE PROMISED YOU."	ISAIAH 54:17, "NO WEAPON THAT IS FORMED AGAINST YOU WILL PROSPER; AND EVERY TONGUE THAT ACCUSES YOU IN JUDGMENT YOU WILL CONDEMN. THIS IS THE HERITAGE OF THE SERVANTS OF THE LORD, AND THEIR VINDICATION IS FROM ME," DECLARES THE LORD."
ISAIAH 40:31, "BUT THEY WHO WAIT FOR THE LORD SHALL RENEW THEIR STRENGTH; THEY SHALL MOUNT UP WITH WINGS LIKE EAGLES; THEY SHALL RUN AND NOT BE WEARY; THEY SHALL WALK AND NOT FAINT."	ZECHARIAH 4:6, "THIS IS THE WORD OF THE LORD TO ZERUBBABEL: 'NOT BY MIGHT NOR BY POWER, BUT BY MY SPIRIT,' SAYS THE LORD ALMIGHTY."
PSALM 44:4-5, "YOU ARE MY KING AND MY GOD, WHO DECREES VICTORIES FOR JACOB. THROUGH YOU WE PUSH BACK OUR ENEMIES; THROUGH YOUR NAME WE TRAMPLE OUR FOES.	JOHN 10:10 NIV - THE THIEF COMES ONLY TO STEAL AND KILL AND DESTROY; I HAVE COME THAT THEY MAY HAVE LIFE, AND HAVE IT TO THE FULL.
DEUTERONOMY 3:22, "DO NOT BE AFRAID OF THEM; THE LORD YOUR GOD HIMSELF WILL FIGHT FOR YOU."	ROMANS 8:31, "WHAT THEN SHALL WE SAY TO THESE THINGS? IF GOD IS FOR US, WHO IS AGAINST US?"

ACTION PLAN

OUR WEAPONS AGAINST THE PROBLEMS OF THIS WORLD

PHILIPPIANS 2:10-11, "THAT AT THE NAME OF JESUS EVERY KNEE SHOULD BOW, IN HEAVEN AND ON EARTH AND UNDER THE EARTH, AND EVERY TONGUE ACKNOWLEDGE THAT JESUS CHRIST IS LORD, TO THE GLORY OF GOD THE FATHER."

2 CORINTHIANS 10:4-5, "THE WEAPONS WE FIGHT WITH ARE NOT THE WEAPONS OF THE WORLD. ON THE CONTRARY, THEY HAVE DIVINE POWER TO DEMOLISH STRONGHOLDS. WE DEMOLISH ARGUMENTS AND EVERY PRETENSION THAT SETS ITSELF UP AGAINST THE KNOWLEDGE OF GOD, AND WE TAKE CAPTIVE EVERY THOUGHT TO MAKE IT OBEDIENT TO CHRIST."

ISAIAH 53:5, "BUT HE WAS PIERCED FOR OUR TRANSGRESSIONS, HE WAS CRUSHED FOR OUR INIQUITIES; THE PUNISHMENT THAT BROUGHT US PEACE WAS ON HIM, AND BY HIS WOUNDS WE ARE HEALED."

JEREMIAH 1:10, "SEE, TODAY I APPOINT YOU OVER NATIONS AND KINGDOMS TO UPROOT AND TEAR DOWN, TO DESTROY AND OVERTHROW, TO BUILD AND TO PLANT."

GALATIANS 5:1, "IT IS FOR FREEDOM THAT CHRIST HAS SET US FREE. STAND FIRM, THEN, AND DO NOT LET YOURSELVES BE BURDENED AGAIN BY A YOKE OF SLAVERY.

REVELATIONS 5:10, "YOU HAVE MADE THEM TO BE A KINGDOM AND PRIESTS TO SERVE OUR GOD, AND THEY WILL REIGN ON THE EARTH."

ISAIAH 61:3, " AND PROVIDE FOR THOSE WHO GRIEVE IN ZION– TO BESTOW ON THEM A CROWN OF BEAUTY INSTEAD OF ASHES, THE OIL OF JOY INSTEAD OF MOURNING, AND A GARMENT OF PRAISE INSTEAD OF A SPIRIT OF DESPAIR. THEY WILL BE CALLED OAKS OF RIGHTEOUSNESS, A PLANTING OF THE LORD FOR THE DISPLAY OF HIS SPLENDOR.

ISAIAH 10:27, "IN THAT DAY THEIR BURDEN WILL BE LIFTED FROM YOUR SHOULDERS, THEIR YOKE FROM YOUR NECK; THE YOKE WILL BE BROKEN BECAUSE YOU HAVE GROWN SO FAT."

PSALM 55:22, "CAST YOUR CARES ON THE LORD AND HE WILL SUSTAIN YOU; HE WILL NEVER LET THE RIGHTEOUS BE SHAKEN."

MATTHEW 11:28-30, "COME TO ME, ALL YOU WHO ARE WEARY AND BURDENED, AND I WILL GIVE YOU REST. TAKE MY YOKE UPON YOU AND LEARN FROM ME, FOR I AM GENTLE AND HUMBLE IN HEART, AND YOU WILL FIND REST FOR YOUR SOULS. FOR MY YOKE IS EASY AND MY BURDEN IS LIGHT."

ACTION PLAN

OUR WEAPONS AGAINST THE PROBLEMS OF THIS WORLD

DEUTERONOMY 5:9, "YOU SHALL NOT BOW DOWN TO THEM OR WORSHIP THEM; FOR I, THE LORD YOUR GOD, AM A JEALOUS GOD, PUNISHING THE CHILDREN FOR THE SIN OF THE PARENTS TO THE THIRD AND FOURTH GENERATION OF THOSE WHO HATE ME."

EXODUS 12:13, "THE BLOOD WILL BE A SIGN FOR YOU ON THE HOUSES WHERE YOU ARE, AND WHEN I SEE THE BLOOD, I WILL PASS OVER YOU. NO DESTRUCTIVE PLAGUE WILL TOUCH YOU WHEN I STRIKE EGYPT."

ZECHARIAH 2:5, "AND I MYSELF WILL BE A WALL OF FIRE AROUND IT,' DECLARES THE LORD, 'AND I WILL BE ITS GLORY WITHIN.'"

JOHN 16:13, "BUT WHEN HE, THE SPIRIT OF TRUTH, COMES, HE WILL GUIDE YOU INTO ALL THE TRUTH. HE WILL NOT SPEAK ON HIS OWN; HE WILL SPEAK ONLY WHAT HE HEARS, AND HE WILL TELL YOU WHAT IS YET TO COME."

LUKE 18:7-8, "AND WILL NOT GOD BRING ABOUT JUSTICE FOR HIS CHOSEN ONES, WHO CRY OUT TO HIM DAY AND NIGHT? WILL HE KEEP PUTTING THEM OFF? I TELL YOU, HE WILL SEE THAT THEY GET JUSTICE, AND QUICKLY. HOWEVER, WHEN THE SON OF MAN COMES, WILL HE FIND FAITH ON THE EARTH?"

EPHESIANS 6:11-12, "PUT ON THE FULL ARMOR OF GOD, SO THAT YOU CAN TAKE YOUR STAND AGAINST THE DEVIL'S SCHEMES. FOR OUR STRUGGLE IS NOT AGAINST FLESH AND BLOOD, BUT AGAINST THE RULERS, AGAINST THE AUTHORITIES, AGAINST THE POWERS OF THIS DARK WORLD AND AGAINST THE SPIRITUAL FORCES OF EVIL IN THE HEAVENLY REALMS. "

1 JOHN 3:8, "HE THAT COMMITTETH SIN IS OF THE DEVIL; FOR THE DEVIL SINNETH FROM THE BEGINNING. FOR THIS PURPOSE THE SON OF GOD WAS MANIFESTED, THAT HE MIGHT DESTROY THE WORKS OF THE DEVIL."

JAMES 4:7, "SUBMIT YOURSELVES, THEN, TO GOD. RESIST THE DEVIL, AND HE WILL FLEE FROM YOU."

1 JOHN 4:4, "YOU ARE FROM GOD, LITTLE CHILDREN, AND HAVE OVERCOME THEM; BECAUSE GREATER IS HE WHO IS IN YOU THAN HE WHO IS IN THE WORLD."

LUKE 10:19, "BEHOLD, I HAVE GIVEN YOU AUTHORITY TO TREAD ON SERPENTS AND SCORPIONS, AND OVER ALL THE POWER OF THE ENEMY, AND NOTHING SHALL HURT YOU."

2 THESSALONIANS 3:3, "BUT THE LORD IS FAITHFUL, AND HE WILL STRENGTHEN YOU AND PROTECT YOU FROM THE EVIL ONE."

ROMANS 8:37, "IN ALL THESE THINGS, WE ARE MORE THAN CONQUERORS THROUGH HIM WHO LOVED US."

SECTION 7

WHAT'S NEXT

A great door has opened to you. Don't miss this opportunity. You have been chosen by God to walk with Him and do the things that He has determined before time began. You were born in this time and season for such a time as this. Be prepared to move with Him as He leads you to your next steps.

WHAT'S NEXT

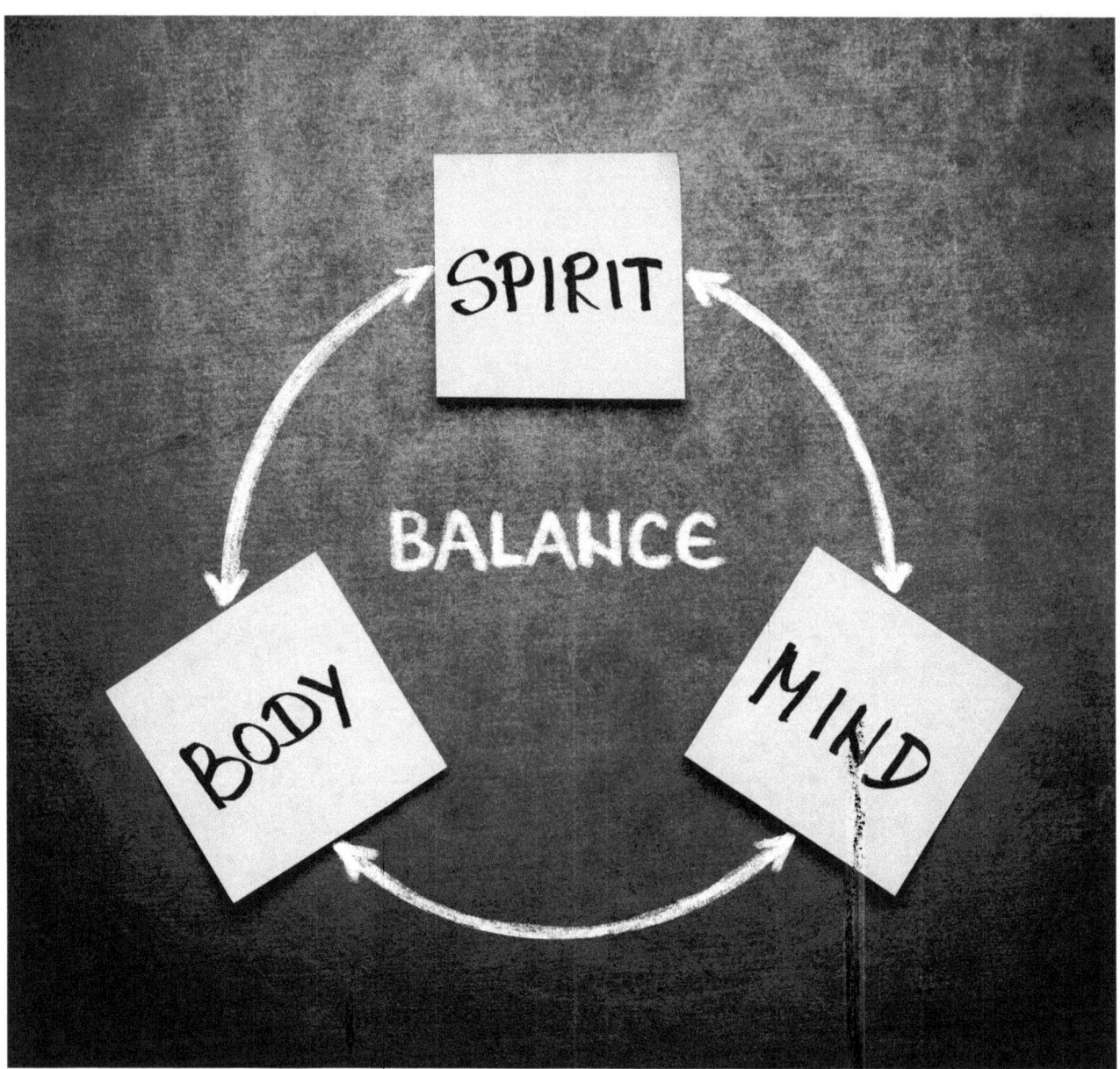

In life, it's easy to get out of balance. The Lord Jesus wants us to learn how to obtain harmony. This requires us to understand the priorities of life and what order things should go in. Jesus said, "Seek first the kingdom of God and His righteousness, and all these things shall be added to you." The following pages are exercises for you to complete that help you place priority based on your culture, lifestyle and family choices.

224

BRAINSTORMING

WHAT IS GOD CALLING YOU TO DO?

VISION BOARD

There's no right or wrong way to complete this exercise. It is for you to think through the things that are important to you so that you begin to plan appropriately to achieve your goals. Don't ever leave God out of those plans. He knows what's best for you and will lead you on the path to achieve them.

SPIRITUAL GOALS **HEALTH GOALS** **CAREER GOALS**

FAMILY GOALS **LIFESTYLE GOALS** **WEALTH GOALS**

GOAL SETTING

From the Vision Board exercise, begin to hone in on SMART goals. Those are specific, measurable, achievable, realistic and time-bound so that you can see light at the end of the tunnel. This exercise will bring clarity to your vision.

S — **SPECIFIC:** What do you want to achieve?

M — **MEASURABLE:** How will you know when you have reached your goal?

A — **ACHIEVABLE:** Is the goal within your power to accomplish?

R — **REALISTIC:** Can you realistically achieve your goal?

T — **TIME-BOUND:** When do you want to achieve your goal by?

227

WHEEL OF LIFE

The wheel of life is a visual tool used to assess and determine how balanced your life is. You start off by determining each area of your life (these can be the most important areas of your life and the roles you have) and mark these out on the wheel below. Evaluate each category and score from 1 to 5 (1 being the lowest) and then connect the dots.

DATE

SCORE

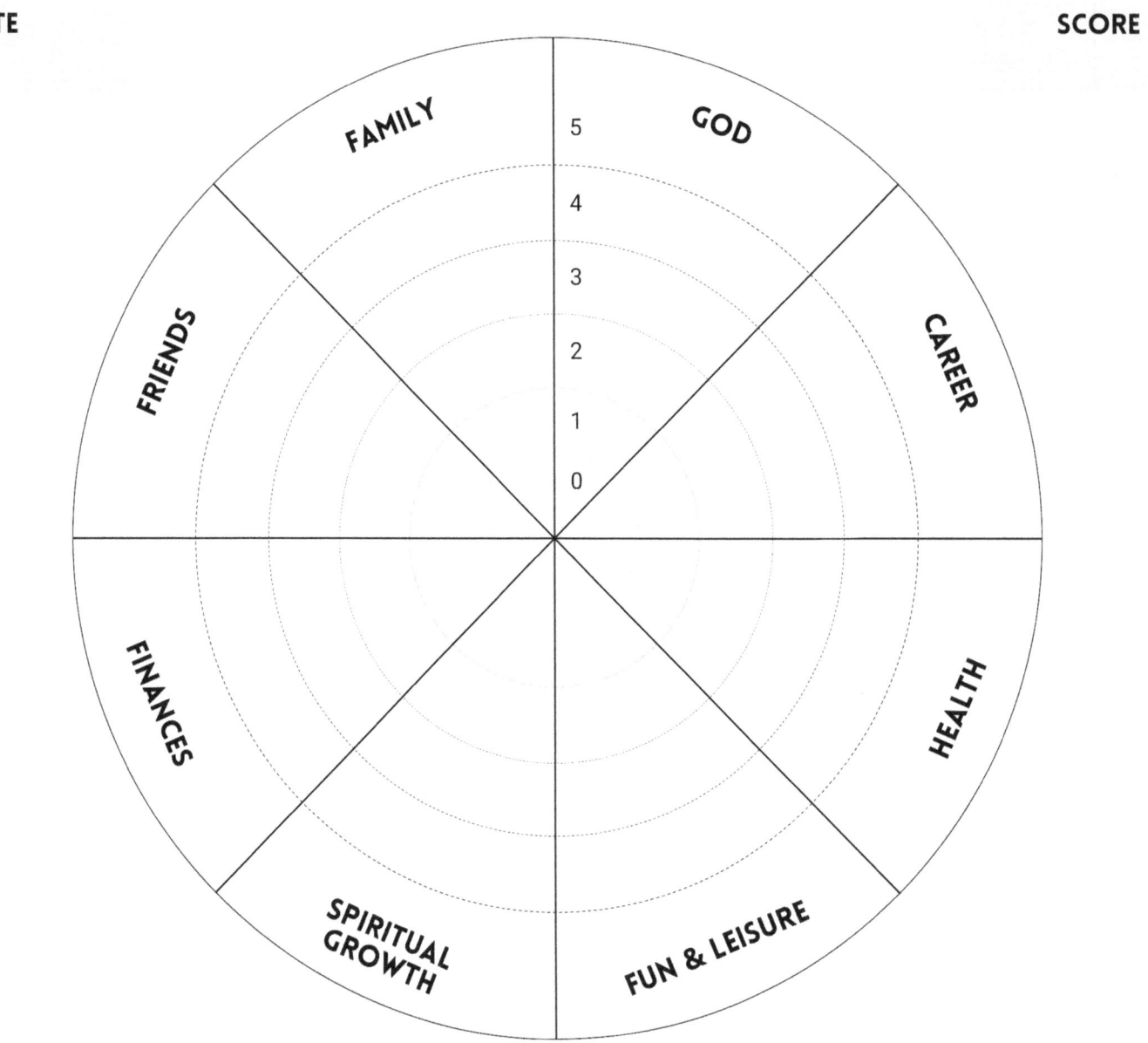

7 DAY PRAYER CHALLENGE

Go with us on a 7-day prayer challenge. Every day of the 7 days has a different focus. You can change some of these to fit your needs or the needs of others that you would like to pray for. Tailor it as you are led to. The goal is to develop the habit of prayer.

DAY 1

PRAYER FOR YOUR FAITH

As you pray, be open to hear what the Spirit of God is saying to you, then write down what you hear.

DAY 2

PRAYER FOR FAMILY

As you pray, be open to hear what the Spirit of God is saying to you, then write down what you hear.

DAY 3

PRAYER FOR YOUR CAREER

As you pray, be open to hear what the Spirit of God is saying to you, then write down what you hear.

DAY 4

FAST & PRAY FOR 24 HOURS

Write a list of things you want to pray for during this time so that you pray them every hour of the day.

DAY 5

PRAYER FOR YOUR COMMUNITY

These prayers can be local, statewide, or for your nation.

DAY 6

PRAYER FOR YOUR FINANCES

Be specific on what you need help with. Maybe you need to curtail your spending. Be transparent with God.

DAY 7

PRAYER FOR THOSE IN NEED

Find those in your area that need help in some way. Pray for their needs to be fulfilled by God.

229

DAILY PLANNER

TODAY'S PRIORITIES

1. _____
2. _____
3. _____

DATE:

IMPORTANT REMINDERS

_____
_____
_____
_____

TODAYS SCHEDULE

8:00 AM

9:00 AM

10:00 AM

11:00 AM

12:00 PM

1:00 PM

2:00 PM

3:00 PM

4:00 PM

5:00 PM

6:00 PM

6:00 PM

MEALS OF THE DAY

BREAKFAST

LUNCH

DINNER

NOTES

230

HABIT TRACKER

MO TU WE TH FR SA SU

HABIT:

MONTH OF:

MY 'WHY':

MY REWARD:

MO TU WE TH FR SA SU

HABIT:

MONTH OF:

MY 'WHY':

MY REWARD:

MO TU WE TH FR SA SU

HABIT:

MONTH OF:

MY 'WHY':

MY REWARD:

PROGRESS TRACKER

Your progress is between you and God but this worksheet is designed to give you a point of reference to take a look back to see your progress over time. Make copies if you need to so that you personalize it to your needs.

TASK: _____   **DEADLINE:** _____

PROGRESS	0%	20%	60%	80%	100%

1st Goal: _____

2nd Goal: _____

3rd Goal: _____

4th Goal: _____

5th Goal: _____

6th Goal: _____

7th Goal: _____

DEVELOPMENT

WHAT ELSE IS THE SPIRIT OF GOD SPEAKING TO YOU?

You may want to sit silently for a while in order to do this exercise. Until you are comfortable with marking and hearing the voice of God, this is a great way to determine who's speaking. If the voice is loud and gets louder, it's probably not God's voice. Holy Spirit speaks in a still, small voice and at times may sound like your voice.

DEVELOPMENT

Now that you've gone through this course, there may be other things that you struggle with as you are developing in your walk with God or you need advice on other life matters. I want to hear about them.

LIST OTHER COURSES THAT YOU WOULD LIKE US TO DO.

This does not have to be limited to spiritual matters. I've worked in all facets of business and can be of assistance in many ways. Let me know specifically how we can assist you.

LIST 5 PEOPLE THAT CAN BENEFIT FROM THIS COURSE.

If possible, please provide their names, their contact information, unless they prohibit it.

It's important that once you have been set free from the weight of sin and the root cause of it, which is the offenses that come from Leviathan, that you remain free. Once you get out, stay out. Never return to life stricken by the enticement of Leviathan by being offended by any and everything that can come against you. Stay attuned to the Holy Spirit because He will help you to see clearly the path to stay free. Leviathan is tricky and uses all types of methods to trip us up. Don't let him and don't be deceived. Nothing is worth going back to that life of imprisonment.

Your identity in Christ is sure, so be confident of God's protection and safety as you move ahead. Knowing who you are and whose you are is the key to unlock the kingdom's arsenal of weapons that can be used to exercise your dominion in the earth. Sin took it away, but the Blood of Jesus forced dominion to be returned to us.

KEY TAKEAWAYS

- Be sure of your identity in Christ.
- As a believer, learn to use the keys of the Kingdom.
- Remember, all of heaven is backing you up, when you follow Christ.
- As you become a student of Jesus, keep balance in your life.

235

PRAYER REQUEST

NEED PRAYER?

Now that you have completed this master class, you may have prayer requests that you didn't have before. We are always here to pray for and with you as you grow in your relationship with Christ. Through our online presence, we want to build a community of prayer warriors that work in unity with the Holy Spirit to pray for those in need. If you feel led to participate with us, please sign up on our website. We look forward to welcoming you into the movement.

FINAL THOUGHTS

- IT'S TIME TO OPEN THE GATES TO LET THE KING OF GLORY IN.

- DEVELOP & MAINTAIN DOMINION

- REEVALUATE & TEST YOUR PLAN

- DO THE WORK

- SHORTCUTS DON'T EXIST HERE

- SAVOR YOUR PROGRESS WHEN IT HAPPENS

- FORGET ABOUT WHAT OR WHO BROKE YOU

- REWARD & REGISTER THE BREAKTHROUGHS

- DON'T WASTE THE FAILURES, THEY CREATE OPPORTUNITIES

- MIRACLES MANIFEST WHEN GOD BECOMES THE CENTER OF YOUR EXISTENCE

- WE'RE ALL BECOMING SOMETHING

- FINDING CHRIST IN ME. THAT'S WHAT I AM TO BE.

NOTES

NOTES

YOUR

FEEDBACK

IS IMPORTANT TO US

Did you enjoy this course/ebook? 🙂 We loved it! 😐 As expected 🙁

How would you rate your instructor? ⭐1 ⭐2 ⭐3 ⭐4 ⭐5

What did you most like about this course/ebook?

_____

_____

How likely are you to recommend us to your family & friends?

unlikely **0 1 2 3 4 5 6 7 8 9 10** Definitely!

How would you rate the content and course materials?

Poor   Fair   Acceptable   Good   Excellent

If you have any other comments or suggestions, we would love to hear them below!

RESOURCE GUIDE

Going deeper requires you to have resources at your disposal to help you achieve the goals that you've set. The following are a few that are available.

YOUVERSION BIBLE APP

This is an app that can be downloaded to your mobile device. There are study resources available.

CHOSEN

A memoir written by **Lauraine White** that tells the stories of leaving religion and how we are all chosen by God for something.

THE WAY OUT

Another book written by **Lauraine White** that speaks to the church at the pinnacle of change and how God, once again comes to the rescue.

HOW TO STUDY THE BIBLE FOR BEGINNERS

This is a great resource for beginners written by **HowExpert Press** and can be found on Amazon.

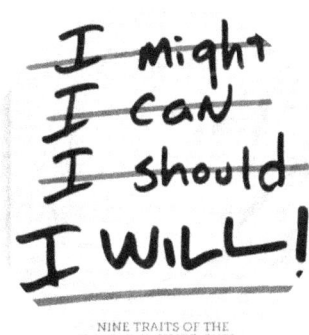

I WILL

This book written by **Thom Rainer** shares that the answers to the worlds problem is for all of us to answer.

NOT A FAN.

In a world where most want to increase their fans, **Kyle Idleman**, speaks to Jesus wanting followers, not fans.

241

JOIN THE MOVEMENT!

AND BECOME A PART OF THE TRIBE TODAY!

We're building a community of believers that stand on the word of God that says we are a chosen generation that will perform the greater works that Jesus said that we would. If you agree with this mission, please consider joining our community as we connect our faith for the impossible to become possible. We look forward to seeing you at other courses, either on Zoom or live and in person at our retreats and other events. Stay tuned.

MIRACLE MOVEMENT

BOOKS WRITTEN BY LAURAINE WHITE

Chosen

Originally published in 2016, Lauraine White pushes the bar while telling much of her life's story. She tells of how God opened a door for her to witness, first hand, the inner workings of international ministries in order for her to see the new age of idol worship. It was and always will be an abomination.

The Way Out

After some very traumatic events in her life, Lauraine White, needed a way out. This story, inspired by those events, is told along with how she got out. The message is simple and clear. Jesus is our only way out.

Bulletproof

Inspired by a dream, Lauraine White delivers a call to action message to the Church to come back to its first love and do the work that it is called to do, especially in times like these when many have fallen away from the Truth.

MASTER CLASSES OFFERED

THE WAY OUT MASTER CLASS

Prepare to embark on a journey of discovery. You are here by divine design and being called to God's Army. This call requires that you be equipped with not just any weapons but by those that make demons quiver.

In this workbook, Lauraine shares exercises that will push you to prepare a workable life plan. The work you will do will launch you into your destiny. You will laugh, cry, and realize that you are meant for so much more than what you thought. God's original plans for your life begins now.

BULLETPROOF MASTER CLASS

A prolific writer and speaker, Lauraine White comes with a bold project-Bulletproof Master Class to educate and equip believers in Jesus Christ. These lessons enlighten students on how to overcome the battles brought on by our adversary, Satan. Through bible study and practical exercises, Lauraine leads her students to understand the keys of the Kingdom of Heaven that gives us authority over all the powers of Satan. When this is understood, dominion on earth can be realized. These processes are tried and true methods she used, under the direction of the Holy Spirits to find her own way out of some very dark places. Prepare to be challenged and motivated to see Jesus in a whole new way. He's worth a second look.

NOTES

NOTES

LEAVE US A
REVIEW

We hope you enjoyed our Master
Class and found lots of value to
help you! We would appreciate if
you wouldn't mind taking the
time to leave us a review.
Thanks!

Lauraine White

<u>*www.miracle-movement.com*</u>

<u>Limits of Liability and Disclaimer of Warranty</u>

Cover Design by: Veezie Forbes Design Studio, Atlanta, GA
Photography by: Neiko James of Chris Perfect Studios & Gerren K. Clark

BULLETPROOF MASTERCLASS

BY LAURAINE WHITE
MIRACLE-MOVEMENT.COM

GET IN TOUCH

 INFO@MIRACLE-MOVEMENT.COM

 + 1 770.912.3894

 @MIRACLEMOVEMENT

 MIRACLEMOVEMENT

BULLETPROOF MASTERCLASS

BY LAURAINE WHITE